Do You Enjoy God?

12 Steps to Enjoying God Everyday

By Pete Rogers

Do You Enjoy God? 12 Steps to Enjoying God Everyday

Acknowledgments

Every author has a team behind them to get their work to press and to the market. I am no different. I would be remiss if I didn't mention the team behind me getting this work into your hands. First is my wife, Susan. You have encouraged me and inspired me to seek God and to know Him intimately. Thank you for being my partner through this journey.

Next, is my editor, Lisa Greenway, truly a woman after God's own heart. Lisa is perhaps the kindest person I have ever known. Her words of encouragement, support and guidance have transformed my writing. She is one of the biggest reasons this book is complete and ready for you to read. I am thankful for her every day. She has been more than an editor, but also a dear friend. Thank you, Lisa. I look forward to many more projects together.

Last but not least, I want to thank God for giving me the determination to pound words onto a page and the ideas to capture. I am driven by the awe I feel for God and his amazing love for me. His love for me is everlasting and undeserved, and it is because of His grace that I am who I am. Through the task of writing this piece, I felt His presence and comfort, and I know the words came from Him. I learned a lot in putting this together, and mostly, I learned how to fully enjoy God every day. It is my prayer and hope that you, too, will experience Him and enjoy Him every day.

Copyright © 2021 by Pete Rogers

All rights reserved. No part of this book, either in part or in whole, may be reproduced, transmitted or utilized in any form or by any means, electronic, photographic or mechanical, including photocopying, recording, or by any information storage and retrieval system, without permission in writing from the publisher, except for brief quotations embodied in literary articles and reviews.

Requests for permission to make copies of any part of this book should be made to:

Pete Rogers Outdoors
251 W. McElhaney Road
Taylors, SC 29687

Cover Art
"Finally Free"
by Darby Adair O'Brien
Courtesy of John and Kelly O'Brien and Family

International Standard Book Number: 978-1-7320266-6-7

Do You Enjoy God? 12 Steps to Enjoying God Everyday

Preface

In the Westminster Shorter Catechism , question 1 reads:
Q: "What is the chief end of man?"
A: "Man's chief end is to glorify God, and to enjoy Him forever."

<u>Paraphrase</u>: What is the purpose of Humanity? Why am I here? For what reason was I created? What is the meaning of life?

For centuries humanity has searched for this answer. Most people would agree that humanity has some connection with God. For those of us who consider ourselves spiritual people, or people of faith, on some level, we have some sort of inkling within us that allows us to believe on some elementary level. As I have strived to understand the first question of the shorter catechism, I have come to understand that people for millennia have acknowledged God, tolerated God, or feared God. Some have loved God, worshipped God, and strived to understand God. But few of us, very few of us actually, <u>enjoy</u> God. And when we do find ourselves in the *moment* of enjoying God, it is usually fleeting at best. God answered our prayers. A loved one survived against all odds. A dream was realized, a sunrise was embraced, and God is enjoyed for a brief moment. But how do we take those fleeting moments and make them last? How can we as humans learn to enjoy God every day? What can we do to ensure that we, as humans, are able to embrace our God in such a way that we not only acknowledge Him, but we genuinely enjoy Him every day? This book will attempt to answer that one question.

Anthropologists have reported for centuries that every culture that has ever been studied has at its core two primary questions that they try to answer within their belief system: 1. What is the meaning of life? and 2. What happens when we die?

While these questions are at the center of Judaism and Christianity, we will attempt to look at only the first one in this book. Hopefully, gaining a unique understanding of what our real purpose is and more importantly, how to fulfill and enjoy that purpose.

When I first read the lines from the shorter catechism, I had a similar experience as John Wesley describes in his journal when hearing the reading of Martin Luther's preface of the letter to the Romans. Wesley said, "When I heard the reading, I felt my heart strangely warmed, and I knew with certainty that Christ did indeed die just for me." While my realization wasn't a salvific experience, it certainly opened the door to a greater understanding of why I am here, and I believe, more importantly, it was more of a moment of enlightenment. It was, in fact, an epiphany, a moment of assurance, and a challenge. How can someone truly *enjoy* God forever? I wasn't sure, at first, if I'd ever really *enjoyed* God at all. So how could a life be spent enjoying him forever? We have all heard sermons and bible studies that tell us that we should glorify God, worship God and praise God. Admittedly, I'd never heard nor preached a sermon with a concept of *enjoying* God. How could we truly enjoy God in our every day?

As I studied this concept, I came to the realization that if we do truly glorify God, we can then enjoy God. If we worship God, then we will enjoy God. If we give praise to God, we will then enjoy God. If we are to honor God, we will enjoy God. If we follow God, we will enjoy God. If we love God, we will enjoy God. When we pray to God, we enjoy God. When we walk with God, we enjoy God. But in a practical, everyday routine, how do we practice living and enjoying God?

As the Psalmist says, "Blessed is the one who does not walk in step with the wicked or stand in the way that sinners take or sit in the company of mockers, **2** but whose delight is in the law of the LORD, and who meditates on his law day and night." (*New International Version*, Psalm 1:1-2) We can delight in the law of God and in the mercy of God. In order to fully enjoy God, we have to have some understanding of what God intends for our life and for our future. This book will look at the many ways God reveals himself to us so that we can have fullness and peace with Him.

Do You Enjoy God? 12 Steps to Enjoying God Everyday

Table of Contents

1. Where Does it Begin?   13
2. Created in God's Image   21
3. Discovering Your Gifts   29
4. Living, Not Merely Existing   37
5. Realizing the Miracles in Your Life   47
6. Enjoying God during Trying Times   55
7. Enjoying God in the Daily Struggles   63
8. Finding Happiness   71
9. Enjoying God in Worship   83
10. Enjoying God in the Outdoors   95
11. Recognizing God in your Life   103
12. Conclusion   115

About the Author   119

Do You Enjoy God? 12 Steps to Enjoying God Everyday

1

Where Does It Begin?

Since the beginning, humankind has sought a relationship with his or her creator. From the most remote places to the most populated – from jungles to deserts, from isolated islands to metropolitans. Every civilization, regardless of how crude they seem to be, is searching for the meaning of Life. Mayans, Incas, Sioux, Apache and Cherokee all have a belief system that gives them purpose. Mongolians, Africans, Amazonian's, Pacific Islanders and Anglo-Saxons all have a belief system that is rooted in two questions that gives them meaning for being. Humanity everywhere is seeking meaning and understanding.

Christians are no different. For us, our story begins in the Garden of Eden and ends at the final reign of Christ that is yet to occur. The one thing that separates us from all other belief systems is relationship. Muslims don't have an ongoing relationship with Allah or Muhammad. Buddhists don't have a relationship with Buddha. Hindus don't have a relationship with any of their gods. No other religion in the existence of humanity can claim an active relationship with its creator.

Christians are the only people of faith that have an active

relationship with their God. Think about that. The creator of all things - heavens and earth, stars and planets, plants and animals - wants a relationship with you!

What does it really mean to "have a relationship" with Jesus Christ? As people who live in community, we have a variety of relationships. Some of the relationships I have are child, brother, husband, father, uncle, employee, coach, umpire, friend, teacher, student, parishioner, teammate, colleague, neighbor, among others.

Each of these relationships is different from one another. Each relationship is unique; each one requiring different responsibilities and different responses from me. Each relationship I am in requires something different from me, something that is unique to that individual or group.

Somehow, in most of these relationships, we know how to behave and respond. In others we learn how to respond. I didn't have to learn how to be a child. But being a husband was a learned process. I didn't have to learn how to be an uncle. But being a daddy, well, that's another story. And I am certain my children would say one I am still learning.

As a husband and father, I have unique relationships with my wife and my children. The relationship I have with my wife is very different than the relationship I have with my children. Both are valuable. Both are fulfilling, and both are necessary for me to live completely and to be whole. But they are very different from one another.

As a husband, I am tasked with being a partner with my wife, to love her, believe in her, support her and take care of her. I am tasked by scripture to love her as Christ loves the church. And to provide for her a safe place to live and to share in our experiences. My role as a husband demands that I lead my wife spiritually. That I drive the efforts for spiritual growth in the relationship. It demands that I put God first and her second. That we pray together, worship together and grow together.

As a father, I have a different relationship with my children. I am told in scripture that I am to rear them to love and fear (respect) God. I am told that it is my job to help them to understand the love He has for them. I am to instruct them in the ways of scripture and to encourage them, teach them, love them unconditionally. While there is significant overlap with these relationships, they are uniquely different.

Similarly, my relationship with my mother is different from other relationships. As her youngest child we have a different relationship, and this one has evolved through time. From parent – child to parent – adult-child, while she continually reminds me that I will always be her baby. As an adult, our roles are very different than when I was a child. As long as she is alive, I will always be her youngest child – and in her eyes that is where I stay. But reality is that now as she moves into the later stages of life, the roles have reversed, my siblings and I are the care givers and she the care receiver. But the relationship with my mother is unique to me as an individual.

The relationships we have with our siblings, our cousins, our employers, friends and acquaintances are all important and yet very different from one another. I have many relationships that I treasure, many that I value very highly. I have others that are important to me, but honestly, if I lost them, they wouldn't be missed at the same degree as others.

All of these relationships we have are important to our make-up, to our happiness, to our living fulfilled lives. I don't believe for a second God intended for people to live outside of relationships. We are not intended to be isolated hermits. We are community people who find happiness and completeness in relationships. That's why when relationships end, we are hurt. We are left feeling empty. We go through feelings of isolation.

When someone we love begins to leave us, or dies, we are hurt and feel abandoned. The life God created is for us to live together in relationship with Him and with one another.

Thus, our relationship with God is a unique relationship also. We cannot compare our relationship with God and Jesus Christ to any other relationship we are in. Our relationship with God cannot be compared to a marriage relationship. And while the scripture makes some references to father/child. It's still not quite that either. It's better than that, and it's different from that.

All relationships we have, we choose to either endure them or enjoy them.

That being said, how do we really enjoy our relationship with God?

When we come to the realization that Christ died for us and we accept for ourselves the offer for salvation, we then accept His invitation to enter into a relationship with Him. I liken it to the dating/courting time and then the marriage proposal. Prior to the marriage proposal, we are in a courting relationship; we date girls or guys in hopes of finding a mate. We test the waters, go out to dinner and a movie. And when we feel we are most assured, we bring them home to mom and dad looking for approval. Our relationship with Jesus Christ is similar.

Prior to our acceptance of him (being born again), we are in a courting relationship. The Holy Spirit is courting us, wooing us into relationship. John Wesley termed this the Prevenient Grace of God. It is the grace that comes before; the grace of God that is present in our lives, carrying us, sustaining us and drawing us into relationship with him. It is that Grace that precedes our justification (getting saved) that we experience when we listen to the Holy Spirit and accept for ourselves the offer of salvation (more on this later). This is the courting stage. When the proposal is presented, we accept the offer.

In a marriage proposal we understand that we are accepting (or asking) someone to join with us in a unique relationship that will last "till death". It's a lifetime commitment, a sincere vow that we take understanding that this new relationship we are entering into will change us forever, and we believe for the better. But it takes commitment, adjustment, and a determination that we will get the best out of it because we will put our best into it.

When we enter into the relationship with Jesus Christ, we should enter into it with the same determination, the same resolve, and the same commitment that we will get the most out of it because we put our best into it.

In the third chapter of John, there is a conversation that explains it all for us.

It's a familiar conversation between Jesus and Nicodemus that highlights the importance of relationship for all believers and nonbelievers. In this conversation, Jesus pronounces what are perhaps the most poignant verses in all of scripture and some that we all hold dear. Jesus says in John 3:16, "For God so loved the world that he gave his son that whoever believes in him will not perish but have eternal life." (*New American Standard Bible*).

When Jesus looked at Nicodemus and said, "...whoever believes....," the world changed. People with no hope have hope. People who are hurting have a balm. Those who are living in despair have courage. God changed it all in one simple phrase. One action, one act of love and grace transformed the world in ways we still haven't seen. But for us, for those who accepted the proposal, it changes us forever.

God wants you to become a "WHOEVER." The desire of God and his son Jesus is that everyone, everywhere becomes a "WHOEVER".

The word *WHOEVER* here is very important. No matter who you are or where you are from, the invitation is yours. For Nicodemus, it meant that not just the Jews were acceptable. For us it means that we are acceptable just as we are. As a "WHOEVER," I am okay, I am good enough, I am just fine just as I am. As a "WHOEVER," I don't have to look like you or act like you or be like you. I am who I am because God made me this way. And as such, I know that I can have a relationship with my creator.

When Jesus said to Nicodemus "Whoever believes in me . . .," the game changed. The mold was broken, the restrictions lifted. "WHOEVER" means us *all* - men, women, white, black, Asian, bi-racial, multi-racial, tall, short, thin, fat, smart, challenged, educated, illiterate, whole and broken. We are all welcome. Most importantly, we are loved and valued. God values us all and wants to be a part of our lives completely and absolutely.

Scripture is full of "WHOEVERS." In Mark 11:23 Jesus tells us, "Whoever says to this mountain, 'Be taken up and cast into the sea' and does not doubt in his heart, it shall be granted him." (*New American Standard Bible*). In John 14:12, Jesus tells us, "... whoever believes in me will do the works I have been doing...," and there are more. As a "WHOEVER," you are accepted. You are welcomed, you are loved and most importantly, you are valued! Jesus says to us all, *whoever*, everyone, all people, I want you, I need you, I love you.

As a "WHOEVER," you are relieved of any presupposed expectations, you are relieved of all guilt, all sins are released, and all failures are forgotten. As a "WHOEVER," you are loved just for being alive! You are valued just because you are.

As we seek to *enjoy* God in the everyday, knowing that we are good enough is a great place to start. God doesn't expect saints. He welcomes sinners. He isn't expecting perfection; he is looking for effort. He takes our "fixer-upper" and makes us a mansion. And it all begins with a relationship. A relationship that starts as a "WHOEVER," and we enter into that relationship as we are and continue throughout our lives. It sustains us until we are finally welcomed into His arms.

A relationship with Jesus Christ is where we begin our journey of enjoying God in the everyday. Unlike all other relationships, where we are expected to behave in a certain way. When we are in relationship with Christ, we have no expectations placed on us. We have no requirements. No hurdles to jump before we are accepted. We are accepted because we are His. This relationship is life changing, and it is glorious.

If we have not yet accepted Jesus as our savior, we will never be able to find true happiness, true contentment, and true joy. Without a relationship with Christ, we will never be able to enjoy God. Enjoying life begins with learning how to enjoy God, and we cannot enjoy God without a relationship with his son Jesus Christ.

Become a "WHOEVER" and as you read the rest of this book, you will see that life is best lived when we enjoy God to the fullest.

2

Created in God's Image

In Genesis, chapter 1, God shares His creation story. In this story we see that God created the heavens and earth followed by the rest of creation. Genesis gives us the details of God's creation - stars, heavens, plants, animals, and every living thing on the planet. At the end of each of these creation moments, God says, "It is good." Then at the end of His creation, He makes the decision to "make mankind in our image." In this narrative we see that God said it was "very good." As we look at this, I believe that God is pleased with His creation, and He is pleased with Adam and Eve. The scripture says in Genesis 1:26-27, God said, "Let us make mankind in our image...So God created mankind in his own image..." (New International Version). So, the question bears asking, what does it mean to be made in the image of God?

For millennia this question has been asked. What does it mean to be an image bearer of God? What does it mean to you? As you wake in the morning and stumble into the bathroom, when you look into the mirror, do you see the image of God? When you are driving down the highway trying to put lipstick on, do you see the image of God? More importantly, when you are standing in the 10 items or less line at the grocery store and the person in front of you has a full cart, do you see someone created in the image of God? Is the soccer coach who won't play your kid as much as you think he should an image bearer of the Almighty? Is the teacher who puts your child in detention someone who bears the image of God? As you scream at your husband, who just spilled a glass of sweet tea all over your freshly mopped floor, do you see him as someone who is made in the image of God? Is the bully, the oppressed, the obsessed and the homeless made in the image of God? What about you? Are you made in the image of God? Do you live like it? Do you embrace the fact that when you go out into the world, you are carrying the image of the Creator?

When God created everything there is, He took special care and created you. In His masterpiece of creation, there is one moment, one speck that tells all who see it whose this is. It is the focal point of it all. His canvas has all that is beautiful: flowers, trees, mountains, rivers. In His masterpiece are canyons, rainforests and deserts. There are glaciers and prairies, yet in the center of it all is you.

One of the most important elements of being created in God's image is that above all other creation, God wants and needs a relationship with you. With great care, God created this world and all that is in it. For those of us who pause and look, we see amazing creative artistry in this world. Yet, for all the care there is, He doesn't have nor want a relationship with the river. He does not desire a close bond with the tree or mountain. No, God seeks relationship with the greatest of creation – You.

As image bearers, we have a hard time accepting that we are

created in His image. It is difficult for many of us to look in the mirror and see someone who carries the image of God. But as difficult as this is, many of us have an even harder time accepting that others are also created in His image.

Democrats don't like to admit that Republicans are image bearers of God. Americans might not like to face the idea that Europeans, Asians, or others are also image bearers of God. The poor might look at the wealthy and struggle to see God in them. The educated look at the under educated and see something other than someone in the image of God. The Protestants look at Catholics and struggle to see image bearers of God and vice versa.

We use political ideologies and geographical boundaries to separate us from one another. We choose sides based on dress codes, skin color, and denominational differences. We decide that we are right, and they are wrong because we sing from different hymnals or read from different versions of the Bible. We devalue some because they speak a different language or work different types of jobs. We elevate others because of the neighborhood they live in and ignore others because of their clothes.

A few days ago, a friend came over to our home for a visit. We will call him Jerry to protect his identity. During this visit, the topic of bi-racial couples came up. It seems in our area of the South, we are seeing more and more couples and families of mixed races. Virtually any combination you can imagine. Jerry, being of a generation that lived through the heart of desegregation, was confessing his difficulty with being able to accept the trend of more and more couples of different races dating or even marrying.

It was a difficult conversation. We could tell he was really struggling with the whole concept. As a Christian, Jerry readily admitted that he could not find scriptural references that prohibited bi-racial couples from marrying. His argument was the standard one of creation and God separating the races onto different continents. But again, there was no scriptural reference to this at all.

If scripture were used, and it was, it was from Numbers 12:1, "Miriam and Aaron began to talk against Moses because of his Cushite wife, for he had married a Cushite." A Cushite was from the country of Ethiopia. Moses, a Hebrew, married a black woman from Ethiopia. When Miriam and Aaron spoke against it, God had a meeting with them, and Miriam was stricken with leprosy. The scripture seems clear.

In addition is the lesson from Paul in Galatians 3:28, "There is neither Jew nor Gentile, neither slave nor free, nor is there male and female, for you are all one in Christ Jesus." If we are all one in Christ Jesus, then the issue Jerry and many others are struggling with is moot. We are all image bearers of the creator, and God views us all equally.

Being created in the image of God is not exclusionary. We are not alone. The girl behind the counter at your local store is an image bearer of God. The CEO and the migrant worker are all created with the same care and carry the same blessing. When we look in the mirror, we should see the face of God. Just as important, when we look at others, we should also see the face of God.

How can we enjoy God in the everyday when we won't accept those who are created in His image? How can we enjoy God when we separate ourselves from the greatest of His creation? How can we experience the fullness of God and be in complete relationship with Him when we exclude a significant portion of the family?

Created in God's Image

So, what does it really mean to be created in the image of God? To put it simply, it means we are created like Him in will, intellect and authority. Nothing else in all creation has these abilities or statutes. Being like God in will separates us from all other animals. We have will, or desire, choice, willingness and the ability to consent or refuse.

All other living things in creation act based solely out of instinct and lust. Animals have only two driving forces: survival and procreation. The need to survive is rooted in eating and drinking, whatever it takes to do this. Without thought or planning, animals eat and drink. Secondly is lust or the need to procreate. This is not something that is desired, it is ingrained to do without thought, malice or planning. They breed to make more of their kind. Human beings, conversely, do not have these same instincts.

Sure, we have a desire to survive, but few of us are ever tested to this point in modern society. Outside of remote third world countries, human beings have more than a need to survive. We have in us, the need to thrive. More importantly, we have a will to decide how and when we will do these things. We have choice and our Will gives us the advantage to decide when and how we will attempt to accomplish these things.

Having the intellect of God does not mean we share His level of intellect. It simply means we have the ability to learn and store knowledge unlike any other thing in creation. *Merriam-Webster* defines intellect as "the power of knowing as distinguished from the power to feel and to will: the capacity for knowledge."

Science has proven that other animals can learn. We know this from our pets. While animals can be trained to perform certain tasks on command, the ability to reason and distinguish and recall is unique to those created in God's image.

When God made us in His image, He made the decision to provide us with intellect. We have the capacity to acquire knowledge and to use that knowledge to understand Him more and to enhance our lives for Him.

Lastly is the authority. As stated earlier, being made in the image of God means we are like Him in will, intellect and *authority*. Image bearers have the unique responsibility to rule over all the rest of creation. "God blessed them and said to them, 'Be fruitful and increase in number; fill the earth and subdue it. Rule over the fish in the sea and the birds in the sky and over every living creature that moves on the ground.'" (Genesis 1:28). We have the responsibility to be the caretakers of all He created. Rule, in this sense, is similar to how a King rules over his kingdom. As a servant ruler, we are tasked with caring for and maintaining for the good of all, all of His creation.

You see, being an image bearer of the Almighty is a big responsibility. It requires us to embrace that we are His. It requires that we adhere to His promises and know that we are His.

In order to enjoy God every day, I believe it starts first and foremost with the relationship with Him. Secondly, we must recognize and embrace the fact that we are created in His image. We carry the image of the creator. When we see ourselves in the mirror, we are looking at the signature on His masterpiece. The most perfect of all there is, is you.

When we look into the eyes of others, we need to see that they, too, carry the image of God. They, too, are created in His image and are loved by Him completely. When we get to the point that everywhere we go and all we encounter, we see God. We can then begin the process of enjoying God. Acts 17:26 tells us, "From one man He made all the nations, that they should inhabit the whole earth; and He determined the times set for them and the exact places where they should live."

God determined that you are right here right now for a reason. He placed you here, today for His purpose. When I see people, who are so dissatisfied with their life, I think of this portion of the verse, "…He [God] determined the time set for them and the exact places they should live." (from Acts 17:26). As an image bearer of God, you have relationship with Him, and you are here - right now for Him – to enjoy Him! But mostly, I think of the masterpiece and how creation occurred, and I realize that we, as human beings, are the signature of His masterpiece. We are the most significant of all there is. We are His signature on His masterpiece of creation.

The most famous question of the Westminster Shorter Catechism is the first:

"Q: *What is the Chief end of Mankind?*

A: The chief end of man is to glorify God and to enjoy him forever."

I submit that this cannot be accomplished until and unless we understand that we and everyone around us are created in the image of God. We are the most important of all there is. We are created in the image of God, and thus, we are an image bearer of the Almighty.

3

Discovering Your Gifts and How to Use Them

I must admit that one of my favorite passages in the New Testament comes from 1 Corinthians 12:4-11. The time Paul spends on sharing the gifts of the spirit and explaining them is important and moving. Have you ever wondered what your gifts are? Do you know how to tell? Do you use them for God? Do you use them at all?

Whenever I go speak at churches, one of the topics I really like to discuss are the spiritual gifts of the people at the church. It never ceases to amaze me how many people look at themselves and do not see any gifts. They assume that gifts are related to professional ministry and a calling. When, in fact, the scripture tells us the exact opposite. The scripture tells us that God gives His gifts to everyone, just as He determines.

If we are to experience God daily and enjoy Him daily and forever, we must use our gifts to their fullest. We must identify what our gifts are and use them where we are as best as we can for His good.

Read on to help you identify what your gifts are and how to use them for the common good.

The Bible tells us, "4 There are different kinds of gifts, but the same Spirit distributes them. 5 There are different kinds of service, but the same Lord. 6 There are different kinds of working, but in all of them and in everyone it is the same God at work. 7 Now to each one the manifestation of the Spirit is given for the common good. 8 To one there is given through the Spirit a message of wisdom, to another a message of knowledge by means of the same Spirit, 9 to another faith by the same Spirit, to another gifts of healing by that one Spirit, 10 to another miraculous powers, to another prophecy, to another distinguishing between spirits, to another speaking in different kinds of tongues, and to still another the interpretation of tongues. 11 All these are the work of one and the same Spirit, and he distributes them to each one, just as he determines." (1 Corinthians 12:4-11).

In this passage there are keys that will help us to first determine what our gifts are, and secondly, how to use them for the common good. Determining what your gifts are is really fairly simple. Ask yourself the following:

1. What do I enjoy doing?
2. What am I good at doing?
3. What are my strengths?

I have come to believe after decades of studying this and trying to find God in this passage, that indeed, our gifts are corralled in these three questions. What do I enjoy? What am I good at? And what are my strengths?

Using the common-sense approach, you must ask yourself, "Would God give me a gift of something I really don't enjoy doing?" Are you going to be passionate about something you hate doing? Exactly, so the first is to look at yourself honestly and determine what you enjoy. That is the first step to discovering your gifts.

Here are two examples of how God is using something I enjoy, and I am pretty good at to benefit the common good of His people.

I really enjoy the outdoors. Everything about the outdoors is fascinating and enthralling for me - hunting, fishing, trapping, camping, and hiking. I love it all. How is this a gift from God? It took me a while to realize that it is in these moments that I encounter God uniquely, and therefore, can use those experiences to invite other men into those arenas to experience God. It is in the time outdoors that I am able to write stories about adventure and bring people into a church, conference room and Podcast and share with them the gospel in a way other people cannot do. Using this gift of the outdoors and an understanding of the outdoors, enables me to use what God has given me to offer an invitation to others to find God in the outdoors.

Another element of enjoyment for me is writing. I love to write and have been doing it for some time. My magazine articles have appeared in dozens of magazines and websites. Over 1,000 articles have been published and each of those are opportunities to build trust and a following that will allow me to share the Gospel with them. God is using my writing for hunting and fishing to bring people into the kingdom. He is using my ability to express myself, my feelings and the feelings of others to further His kingdom. Remember, the scripture says He gives the gifts "for the common good." That is, for the good of others, not necessarily for ourselves.

Lastly, what are your strengths? While attending Erskine Theological Seminary, I took advantage of Professor Bob Glick's offer to teach voice to any student who wanted it. During those first few sessions, Prof. Glick asked me, "What do you want to accomplish?" My answer was simple, "I don't want people to run or begin rebuking spirits out of me when I try to sing."

His sigh of relief was evident. "Good," he said. "I was hoping you were not expecting a miracle."

Obviously singing is not a strength of mine. Professor Glick's encouraging taught me that I was spending too much time trying to strengthen a weakness at the peril of my strengths. "Spend more time making your strength stronger, rather than trying to make your weakness tolerable," he said. And with that, my singing career ended, and my focus has since been to recognize my strengths and to work at making them stronger.

Why would a world class runner spend time swimming when he or she should be running? What good does it do for a doctor to spend his days mowing lawns? Or a gifted teacher washing cars all day long?

God gives us all gifts. He wants us to use them to enhance our lives and to benefit his mission.

> "Now you are the body of Christ, and each one of you is a part of it. [28] And God has placed in the church first of all apostles, second prophets, third teachers, then miracles, then gifts of healing, of helping, of guidance, and of different kinds of tongues. [29] Are all apostles? Are all prophets? Are all teachers? Do all work miracles? [30] Do all have gifts of healing? Do all speak in tongues? Do all interpret? [31] Now eagerly desire the greater gifts. And yet I will show you the most excellent way." (1 Corinthians 12:27-31).

This closing of Chapter 12 of 1 Corinthians is really the launching pad to the famous chapter 13 that is used so often to define love between a man and woman. How many weddings have you been to where this was not used as a definition of how people are to love one another? But if we are to look at the scripture closely, I believe we can see that what Paul is referring to is not a romantic love between a man and a woman, rather it is referring to a much higher love - the ability to love as God loves. How can we enjoy God if we are unable or choosing not to love as He loves? Paul tells us these are gifts of the spirit. Gifts that everyone has. And he highlights that the greatest of these gifts is love. The ability to love as God loves draws us closer to Him and enables us to enjoy His goodness.

Though 1 Corinthians chapter 13 is very popular in defining Godly love, one of the most beautiful scriptures of love is found in 1 John chapter 4:

> "7 Dear friends, let us love one another, for love comes from God. Everyone who loves has been born of God and knows God. 8 Whoever does not love does not know God, because God is love. 9 This is how God showed his love among us: He sent his one and only Son into the world that we might live through him. 10 This is love: not that we loved God, but that He loved us and sent his Son as an atoning sacrifice for our sins. 11 Dear friends, since God so loved us, we also ought to love one another. 12 No one has ever seen God; but if we love one another, God lives in us and His love is made complete in us. 13 This is how we know that we live in him and He in us: He has given us of his Spirit.14 And we have seen and testify that the Father has sent his Son to be the Savior of the world.

15 If anyone acknowledges that Jesus is the Son of God, God lives in them and they in God. **16** And so we know and rely on the love God has for us. God is love. Whoever lives in love lives in God, and God in them. **17** This is how love is made complete among us so that we will have confidence on the Day of Judgment: In this world we are like Jesus. **18** There is no fear in love. But perfect love drives out fear, because fear has to do with punishment. The one who fears is not made perfect in love. **19** We love because He first loved us. **20** Whoever claims to love God yet hates a brother or sister is a liar. For whoever does not love their brother and sister, whom they have seen, cannot love God, whom they have not seen. **21** And he has given us this command: Anyone who loves God must also love their brother and sister."

There are a lot of gifts but one spirit – God gives us each gifts to use for different purposes. But the most important part is understanding that the primary purpose of the gifts he gave you is so you can enhance his church and enjoy him.

I believe that when we are in relationship with Jesus Christ, when we embrace being a "WHOEVER," when we look in the mirror and see someone created in the image of God, when we look at others and see image bearers of God, then we are more able to love fully and completely. And when we can love fully and completely, then we are more LIKE GOD because God is Love.

When we do this, our world changes, and the world of others around us changes. We become more pleasant, we become happier and the dirt of Life doesn't stick to us because we are God's.

Discovering Your Gifts and How to Use Them

Discover your gifts! Use your gifts, be more like him, love fully and completely, and your relationship will grow, and you will be closer to really learning how to ENJOY GOD EVERY DAY.

4

Living, Not Merely Existing

"Don't get so busy making a living that you forget to make a life."

This quote has been attributed to Dolly Parton, but also to many others. Regardless of who actually said it, it is an excellent starting point for this next chapter of learning how to enjoy God every day.

My dad and I never really had the best of relationships. We were not estranged; we were just never close. It wasn't until late in life that he found a relationship with Jesus, and I guess prior to that, he never understood my desire to follow a calling.

For whatever reason, for just about as far back as I can remember, my mother was a golf widow. My dad was bitten by the golf bug when I was young, and nothing stood in his way of going to the golf course. I mean nothing! Three or four days a week, he was at the golf course. Weekends saw him gone long before anyone else was up, and he stayed until it was time for supper. Sundays were the same thing. Dad just couldn't stay away from the golf course. Unless the course was closed for inclement weather, he was there.

But even with this addiction to chasing a white ball, one thing that always comes to my mind when thinking about my dad is that he always went to work.

For most of my life, my dad sold insurance. As an independent insurance agent, he was an entrepreneur. As all entrepreneurs know, if you don't work, you don't eat.

I cannot ever remember my dad using a sick day or skipping out of work for any reason. He was always on time and stayed until the day was over.

I never knew how successful he was or wasn't; it was just something that was never discussed. It was a time when parents didn't discuss these things with their children. But we always had what we needed.

Watching my dad work hard instilled in me a desire to work. As a young man I began work at age 14 on neighbors' farms. Watching my dad, I learned you should go to work, make money, use your money wisely and enjoy life. The one question I never had answered was is there more to life besides making a living? Is there more to life besides getting up going to work, coming home, going to bed and doing it again the next day.

From those early days through high school and into college, I have always had at least one job, but usually two or more. I always had at least one full-time job while attending college and even seminary, working 40 hours a week to provide for myself and my family while I was getting my education.

I was not fortunate enough to have my parents pay for my education. As the first person in my family to attend college, I paid my entire way, 100% of it myself with grants, scholarships and loans.

Living, Not Merely Existing

There have been brief interludes of unemployment, but these were brief. When there is a wife and children, you will do whatever you can to take care of them, which often leads to unpleasant jobs. You have to pay your bills while trying to find something better.

Even as I write this, I have two full-time jobs. I always have; it is what I do. If there is idle time, it is best used working rather than idling. As my mother used to say, "Idle hands are the devil's handiwork." Keep busy. Be productive. Make a difference. If you have time to sit around, you have time to be productive. I guess I have never understood those who are not working. As I drive around and see all of the "now hiring" signs, I have to wonder why so many people are not employed doing something until something better comes along. But perhaps, that is just me. This is not to toot my own horn; in fact, I think it is a bit much. As I write this, I see that perhaps I need to dial it back some.

With all of the demands we place on ourselves and that society places on us, we can easily get caught up in the guise of the status we get by focusing on making a living. It becomes a competition among people to see who can earn a better living that the other person.

The score card is kept by which neighborhood you live in, what kind of car you drive, what clothes you wear and what your portfolio says. Opinions are based on hair styles, name brands, and age of cars rather than by who you are as a child of God.

But I believe God wants more for us than just keeping our noses to the grindstone and eking out a living at whatever cost we can. I believe the scripture is clear, if we are to enjoy God, we need to spend as much time making a life as we do making a living. We need to live and not merely exist.

What does it mean to live? What does it mean when I say make a life? For many people, they would answer this question by saying to live is to breathe in and breathe out. Get up in the morning, go to work, come home and repeat the process for forty years. Get married, have children, grow old and die.

Others see living as chasing dreams and pursuing passions. It can be different things for different people. But there are some commonalities in everyone's life that make life worth living and living fully.

What does it mean to *make a living*? This is usually defined as working somewhere and earning an income to support yourself and or your family financially. We talk about *making a living* and refer to our financial prowess. Some make a better living than others. We say, "Oh John, he makes a great living." But does his salary affect his ability to live? Or does it just affect his ability to exist? Or just his ability to acquire more *things*?

How can we *make a living* if we struggle to have a life? If all of our energy is spent earning or making a living, are we really living the life as God intends for us? Are we really living the best possible life if it takes all our efforts to exist? How can we enjoy God when all of our energy is being spent trying to make a living? Is God even a part of our life if our life is consumed with making a living?

Perhaps, we are thinking about it all wrong. Perhaps, we should focus on truly living and not merely existing. In order for us to enjoy God, we must LIVE. To live fully is to enjoy God completely. Can we truly enjoy God if all we are doing is focusing most of our energy on making a living and not focusing on making a life?

Perhaps you trying to make ends meet takes almost all of

"Paul then stood up in the meeting of the Areopagus and said: "Men of Athens! I see that in every way you are very religious. 23 For as I walked around and looked carefully at your objects of worship, I even found an altar with this inscription: TO AN UNKNOWN GOD. Now what you worship as something unknown I am going to proclaim to you. 24 "The God who made the world and everything in it is the Lord of heaven and earth and does not live in temples built by hands. 25 And he is not served by human hands, as if he needed anything, because he himself gives all men life and breath and everything else. 26 From one man he made every nation of men, that they should inhabit the whole earth; and he determined the times set for them and the exact places where they should live. 27 God did this so that men would seek him and perhaps reach out for him and find him, though he is not far from each one of us. 28 'For in him we live and move and have our being.' As some of your own poets have said, 'We are his offspring.'" (Acts 17:22-28.)

your energy and ability to attempt to pay bills. Living fully seems as if it is not possible. But I would surmise that it is possible and indeed easier than you may think.

Working from 7:30-4:30 five days a week is exhausting. Adding to that a second job that begins at 6:00 P.M. until 11:00 P.M. makes little time for anything other than working. How can someone be expected to live when all one has time for is to work?

In the 17th chapter of Acts, Paul is speaking to the counsel at Athens, Greece. At the time they were considered the most learned people in the world. During this time of addressing the

"Men at Athens," Paul addresses some of the most important elements of his ministry.

Paul confronts us head on here. He proclaims that to truly live, we must be in Christ. *"In HIM we Live and Move and have our being"* (emphasis is mine). To live is to be in Christ. To live is to walk daily with Christ. To live is to have Christ as the center of our existence. To live, we must be with Christ all the time, 24/7/365. Paul, again, in 2 Corinthians 5:17 says, "If anyone is in Christ, he is a new creation. The old has gone and the new has come." To live is to embrace the reality that we are new; we are not the same. We are transformed from the old into the new. To be in Christ, we have to grab onto the God of love and not let Him go. Once we have become a WHOEVER, and we are in relationship with Christ, we are not the same. We have been transformed. We are alive as never before.

To be in Christ is to LIVE fully. To be In Christ is to be completely His. And when we are completely His, we are able to enjoy God to his fullest.

Take, for example, Matt Branch. Matt Branch played college football at Louisiana State University. He was a burly 6'6," 305 pound mammoth of a man. As an offensive lineman for LSU Tigers from 2009-2012, Matt was a force to be reckoned with. That all changed in December of 2018 when Matt was with some friends on a duck hunt in Mississippi. While on this duck hunt, he and his buddies were moving to a new location. They had picked up their decoys and someone drove a UTV to pick them up. Matt laid his shotgun into the bed of the UTV with the muzzle pointing at himself. Shortly afterward one of the dogs who was with them to help retrieve the ducks jumped into the bed of the UTV and Matt's shotgun went off, shooting him in the upper left thigh.

In an instant, his life changed. His friends assessed the situation and knew it was bad and rushed him to the road where the ambulance they had called met them. During this time, Matt lost a lot of blood since the arterial artery of his left leg was destroyed.

Matt was taken to a hospital close by and treated, but they soon learned they could not treat him sufficiently, and he was flown to Jackson, Mississippi for more treatments. Matt slipped into a coma and remained there for twelve days. During this time, Matt received over 300 pints of blood, endured 9 surgeries, two amputations and ultimately, lost his left leg at the hip. What began as an ordinary day turned into an extraordinary miracle. Matt died several times during his ordeal. For a total of 22 minutes, his heart stopped beating, and he was clinically dead. Each time, he was revived and brought back. Each time, he survived.

After months in the hospital, enduring more surgeries, prosthetics, and physical therapy, Matt walked out of the hospital three months after his accident.

Matt is clear that this struggle has been a difficult road. Losing a leg at the hip is a difficult transition for anyone. Everything in your life changes, everything. Nothing is easy anymore. During this time of recovery, Matt questioned God, question why he lived, and struggled with the pain, torment and therapy.

But today, Matt is back at work, and still hunts and fishes every time he can. He knows that his accident was caused by his inattention to detail. But he has made the decision to go on living, to live life to the fullest, and to find a way to enjoy God in the process.

Life is too precious to merely exist. Life is too fleeting to spend all of our time making a living and not focusing on making a life. Sure, our daily battles are big. Many of us are facing sick children, broken marriages, infidelity, and unemployment. Others are facing the trauma of death, bankruptcies, and failed business ventures. Some have had their entire life savings stolen through scams or bad decisions. People are facing extremely tough trials daily, and it is hard to enjoy anything. Through no fault of their own, it feels like the world is crashing down all around them.

A few weeks ago, I received some upsetting news. One of the sources I have been writing magazine articles for was closing shop. For the last five years, I have provided stories for them for their website and suddenly without notice, they decided to shut it down. This was a huge financial hit to our family. But mostly it was a career setback. The freelance outdoor writing world is based largely on relationships. Those relationships were closing. My ego and pocketbook were hurt. I was being laid off for nothing I had done. The company just shut down.

Some of you have been through similar circumstances. The plant you've worked at for all of your life is suddenly relocating out of state or out of the country. Through no fault of your own, you are suddenly unemployed. Mortgages to pay, families to feed, and your life is suddenly interrupted. For some of you, you may have been injured and can't work and are finding it difficult to find value in your life as it is now. Others are grieving a loss of a loved one, or as in Matt's situation, an accident has you in recovery for an extended period of time. God knows your struggles, and it is His desire to see you through them.

I took some days to go to my cabin and reflect, pray and seek God. During this time, I threw a big pity party and felt sorry for myself. But I soon realized that wasn't getting me anywhere.

During my prayer time, I decided to focus my attention, not on what I had lost, the money and the connections, the career setbacks, rather I decided I would (try to) focus my attention on all of the blessings I have. I would focus on trying to praise God for all of the blessings I still had, regardless of how small it seemed to the outside world. By focusing my attention on God, I was no longer feeling sorry for myself. As these weeks have turned into months, and months into years, I now realize that God was clearing my calendar so I could get this story written.

This book began seven years ago. An idea came to mind, and I began writing it down. Then life got busy, my freelance writing career began to grow rapidly, and this book got shelved for seven years! Now, as I have been in a spiritual transition phase of my life, this book came back to life. God knew I could never finish this book while continuing to work on the other material. To paraphrase Joseph when he was sold into slavery by his brothers, what you intended for harm, God intended for good. God took a setback and created an opportunity.

To live is to love as God loves. To live fully, is to focus on God, and what He wants for you. To live is to seek God continually, and to know He is not far away. Ever.

To enjoy God, we need to embrace our role in his creation. We are not just loved by God, we are in relationship with God, we are valued by God, we are image bearers of God, and we are alive with God. Want to enjoy God every day? Give Him thanks for everything that you are, for all you do, for all you have. Spend your days in praise and thanksgiving. If you remember it all starts with Him, you can spend most of every day enjoying all He has blessed you with.

5

Realizing the Miracles in Your Life

Miracles are rare. Miracles happen to other people. I have never had a miracle in my life, so why are we talking about them?

Funny thing about miracles is they are a lot more common than we realize and, therefore, we are not giving God the credit He deserves for the miracles He is performing in your life.

We started with a simple question from the Westminster Shorter Catechism that asks:

Q: "What is the Chief end of Man (humanity)?

A: "The chief end of Man is to glorify God and to ENJOY HIM FOREVER." (emphasis mine)

This led to a simple question – what does it mean to *ENJOY GOD?* We followed this with some questions about who God is and how we recognize Him in the world, as well as in our lives.

Do we Enjoy God?   Can we enjoy God?   How do we Enjoy God?

If we have trouble recognizing God, how much more difficult is it to recognize miracles that have occurred in our lives or in the lives of others?

When we talk about miracles of Jesus, there are certain ones that come to mind. First is His virgin birth. How was Jesus conceived except by a miracle? We think of all of the healings of sick and possessed. We think about raising Lazarus from the dead. Many of us remember Jesus walking on water or turning water into wine. What about feeding the thousands of people with just a few fish and bread? Then, there is the resurrection from the dead and subsequently appearing to His disciples.

When we talk about miracles in YOUR LIFE, what are the first things that come to your mind? Most people when posed this question, immediately go to the birth of their children. That is truly a miracle for sure. Seeing life sprout from the body of a woman is a miracle indeed. And to compound this, knowing the child carries the image of God. This little baby has God's thumbprint on his or her life. It's overwhelming and beautiful.

But there are many other miracles that we have all experienced that we do not often think about, miracles that God performs that we have begun to take for granted as just part of life. Sunrises and sunsets. Ocean tides and rivers that flow endlessly, forever. For many, finding your spouse was a miracle. Of all the billions of people on the planet, could it be a miracle that you found one another? Could it be a miracle that your two lives have become so intertwined to build a family? I believe my wife is a miracle. I am convinced that God placed her in my life just when I needed her, and she has fulfilled God's purpose for me. I hope I have done so for her.

Of all the miracles I have been fortunate enough to witness, two stand out in my mind that are not included in those mentioned above. The first is the story of James Roe.

While serving in my first church as a young and inexperienced pastor, I found myself staring at James Roe as he battled

Hodgkin's disease. I was twenty-three years old at the time and had zero experience in such things. James was the treasurer of our church. He was in his mid-30s, married and no children. He and his wife, Debbie, decided not to have children because of his cancer. After 10 plus years of being cancer free, they decided to try and have a child. Sure enough, Debbie soon found herself to be pregnant with a daughter. It was while Debbie was carrying Sarah that James's cancer returned. I still remember vividly when he told me. "Preacher, I need you to pray for me. My cancer has returned, and I am going to have to go into treatment." Simple request for prayer. James was a strong, quiet man.

Of all the people in the many churches I pastored, James was the most talented I have ever known. His big banana fingers could find their place on a mandolin and fiddle like no other. James loved Bluegrass music and played in bands all the time. He loved the mandolin, the fiddle, guitar and even the banjo. James could play them all, and play them all well.

His skills did not stop there. His hobby was restoring cars. He was especially fond of a Karmann Ghia he restored. A full body-off restoration, including an engine rebuild and total body make-over. He painted it bright yellow. It was beautiful.

As James went through his chemotherapy, he began to lose his coloring, his hair and his strength but not his faith or sense of humor. Unlike many who battle that retched disease, James refused to shave his head, preferring to hang onto the little dabs of hair he had left. A few thin strands held on along the back of his head. He loved stroking those few hairs and commenting about his ponytail.

James's treatment went on for several months, and his conditions seemed to be stabilizing but was not any better. It was then

I heard a voice from God.

While preparing for Sunday services, I had my sermon prepared and was ready to go to church when I felt a nudge to open my bible to the book of James chapter 5:14-15.

> Is anyone among you sick? Let them call the elders of the church to pray over them and anoint them with oil in the name of the Lord. 15 And the prayer offered in faith will make the sick person well; the Lord will raise them up.

I read and re-read that passage. That morning in church, I told the congregation what happened. I felt a nudge from God to bring James to church that afternoon and for the church to gather around him and pray for his healing.

Mind you, I was 23 years old. I had never done anything like this before. I was terrified. That afternoon at 3:00, our little country church gathered. We helped James get up the flight of steps that led to the front door of our little church. Making his way to the front of the church, James sat in a chair. James was a quiet man and really didn't like the attention, but he went along with the situation. That afternoon, James was surrounded by nearly 100 of his closest friends and church members.

I read the scripture and simply said, "We are being obedient to God. We are going to anoint James with oil, and we will pray for him. Anyone who would like to pray, please do so. Let's all reach out and touch someone close to you. As we lay hands on James, we pray….." Over the next hour in that little church, we prayed with such a power I have never experienced before – nor since. Hearts poured out to God. Tears flooded the carpet as people pled with God on behalf of James. We were sincere and scared, but hopeful.

Many miracles happened that day. The little church in Taylors, SC came together as they have never before nor since and offered sincere prayers to God. James Roe came and offered himself to God and to the members of his church. And God heard our prayers. The very next week, James went for a PET scan, and there was no cancer found in his body. Not one cell, not one tumor, nothing!

James continued treatment for a few more months to be sure, but he was healed. Completely healed. Later that year, James and Debbie welcomed Sarah into their life, and I was fortunate enough to get to baptize their daughter and unite the family they had always dreamed about.

Many years later, James's cancer returned, and this time he succumbed to the disease. But his life was a witness to God's grace, and God's healing power.

The second story I want to share with you is not quite as dramatic, but just as profound. It begins with a 15-year-old boy with a severe speech impediment. Before I go any further, this young man was me. For some reason, when I began to talk, I developed a stutter. As I grew, the stutter became more severe. So severe, in fact I could not read aloud at all. Conversations were difficult, and as kids can be so mean, the bullying was intense. This caused me to lash out when made fun of. To compound the agony, we moved a lot, and I had to go to different schools and start over again with the bullies. By the time I entered the seventh grade, I had been to five different schools in three states.

Each move meant a new school, a new speech therapist, new tactics, and new lessons on how to speak. It seemed futile and was very frustrating. For those of you who have not had to deal with this issue, I assure you, it is a silent destroyer. In an auditory world, it can be frustrating to try to communicate. We become reclusive and insecure due to the teasing and ridicule we get from peers. Everyone tries to finish your sentences for you. They feel your pain and try to help. It doesn't help. It just exacerbates the situation.

For me, athletics was an outlet. I played both football and baseball. While in high school, I was moved to the quarterback position, but since I couldn't speak clearly, my coach would send in the plays and the receivers would call the plays for me. As a baseball player, I was a catcher and getting to hide behind the mask gave me confidence. I didn't have to look at the crowd and didn't have to speak.

One Sunday morning in church, I felt God tugging on my heart. I felt a calling to the ministry. My first thought was, "I can't talk. How am I going to be a preacher?" I was scared and frustrated with God. Why couldn't he call me to something that didn't require speaking? I felt like it was a cruel move on God's part to call me into a career that involved speaking.

Moving forward a decade or so, God taught me which combinations of words cause me to stumble. I learned to avoid any words with combinations of L and T, such as the word "little" or "literature." I just cannot say those words. Sentence combinations with several *w*'s cause a stutter. For example, asking someone, "Where were you?" is something I cannot do. I have to substitute words for those words and combinations. So, for *little*, I say, "small." For *literature*, I say, "books" or "works." For combinations of words, I rewrite the sentences to avoid the trips and stutters.

As a pastor, I memorized my sermons. I would usually write

the sermon on Thursdays. Then spend the next three days memorizing it from front to back so I would not get stumped and begin to stutter. If I had it memorized, I could say it in a way that would help me to speak clearly and slowly.

Today, people are shocked when I tell them I have a stuttering issue. I still know it is there. Most people cannot see it or hear it, but I feel it in my mouth every time I try to say something. Has God healed me from stuttering? No, but he did heal me of the embarrassment, of the stress, of the fear to speak. Sure, I still get stumped from time to time, but considering where I was to where I am today, God healed me of my stuttering.

For many, this would not be a miracle. It would be the combination of therapy, trial and error and effort. But for me, knowing where I was and where I am today, I know it was a miracle in my life.

I believe we have miracles occur in our lives daily. We have small but powerful miracles daily in our lives. Most go unnoticed, most are not recognized as such. Most are dismissed or ignored as coincidence, happenstance, luck or accident. We cannot recognize them because we are not walking with God daily. We cannot see the action of God in our lives unless we are enjoying God daily. We cannot see the glory of his action in our lives if we are not enjoying what we have now. But when we are focused on God, when we are focused on enjoying God, it is then we start to recognize these events as what they are – Miracles.

Isn't it a miracle that the Creator of the Universe wants to have a relationship with you? Isn't it a miracle that he entrusted us to carry His image? Isn't it a miracle that we have gifts that we can use to further the kingdom? Isn't it a miracle that we are here at all? Isn't it a miracle that the God of creation and grace loves us at all and that we are good enough, just like we are, to be loved by Him? Isn't a miracle that as a "WHOEVER" we are good enough? We do not have to be anything other than whom he created us to be. We cannot earn His love. We can only embrace His love for us.

It's a miracle that you are here today. When you realize that God – the same God that breathed breath into Adam, that parted a sea, that brought Jonah from the whale – the same God that came to life in Jesus, walked on water, died on a cross, and rose again – cares enough about you that he wants an intimate relationship with you - that is a miracle. And it is the greatest miracle.

How do we realize the miracles in our lives? By focusing our everyday on enjoying God to the fullest. Enjoy what God has done for you. Enjoy what God is doing with you, and embrace what God has in store for you.

We haven't even come close to seeing what God will do with us. When we strive to enjoy God, we see God everywhere. We see his power, we see his love and we recognize his Grace.

The greatest miracle of all is that God loves us at all!

6

Enjoying God during Trying Times

Matthew 28:20: "And surely I am with you always, to the very end of the age."
John 14
Psalm 1

I will call her Sarah to protect her identity. Sarah, the mother of two teenage daughters, moved to our area about the same time we did. A chance meeting struck up an instant friendship with her and our family.

Sarah was married, and as far as anyone knew, there was nothing alarming about their marriage. It seemed "normal," whatever that means. There were no signs of anything from the outside. Sarah and her husband had been married for over 23 years when he announced he was leaving her and their daughters for another – man.

At the time, Sarah had recently gone through severe cancer treatment for uterine cancer. Surgeries and treatments were successful, but she was still feeling the effects of the cancer when the announcement came.

Sarah confided in my wife and me about the despair she was feeling. "How can I compete with a man!" she would say. "If he left for another woman, I would think one thing and try and compete for his affection. But he not only left me, he left for a man!" she would say.

For months, Sarah kept this from her daughters. She just told them that their daddy left and did not tell them why.

Being self-employed, Sarah relied on her husband's insurance to cover her medical expenses. She felt trapped. If she divorced him, she'd lose her insurance, and as a cancer survivor, it would be difficult to get coverage anywhere else or be able to afford it.

Through all of this, Sarah has kept her faith in God. She admits, she doesn't understand why all of this happened. And her pain is deep and real. Still, she keeps faith.

Sarah does not have the market cornered on experiencing trying times. We all have our examples of bad things happening. And one thing is for sure, we cannot compare our difficulty with someone else's difficulty.

What is trying to one person, may not be trying to another. What is difficult for one person may not be difficult for another.

The gospel tells us in Matthew 28:20 at the end of His Great Commission, "...And surely I am with you always, even to the end of the age." Again, in John 14, the great chapter where Jesus is comforting the disciples with the promise of the Holy Spirit, in verses 15-18 Jesus says, "If you love me, keep my commands. **16** And I will ask the Father, and he will give you another advocate to help you and be with you forever—**17** the Spirit of truth. The world cannot accept him, because it neither sees him nor knows him. But you know him, for he lives with you and will be in you."

It seems the difficulty is not in the knowing, it is in the receiving. We know God loves us, we know God is there with us, but in the times of trial, it is difficult to *feel* God with us. It is difficult to enjoy God when it feels like our world is crashing down on us.

For Christians, many of us have that one experience that stands out in our lives as a testimony. When someone you know, hear about or love does something that touches you in a profound way, the way they handle the situation touches you and leaves you forever changed. That is the case for me and John and Kelly O'Brien of Greer, SC.

John and Kelly became close friends of ours when our sons ended up on the same little league baseball team. John and Kelly have four children: Darby, Brooks, Delaney and Brody. Darby's personality just lit up every room and venue she entered. Being the oldest, she modeled for her siblings how to live and how to follow Christ. Few young ladies exemplify God's grace and love more than Darby O'Brien.

As John says, "Darby was the light of the family. She inspired us all to be better people."

In 2012, Darby did what so many kids do and headed off to college. She chose Auburn University, which incidentally is John's Alma Mater. Proud parents, for sure. Darby excelled in meeting people and making a difference in the lives of everyone she touched.

Back at home, all was well. The rest of the O'Brien clan went about daily business. When the phone call every parent fears came, it was November 14, 2012. Darby collapsed at school and was rushed to the hospital and was unresponsive. The local hospital made a quick decision to move her to a hospital in Columbus, Georgia.

John and Kelly had started to drive when a friend offered a private plane to take them to Darby's side. The plane re-routed and landed in Columbus, and they rushed to her side.

"We didn't know what was going on, what had happened or what condition she was in. All we knew is she collapsed in the bathroom," John said.

Darby's roommates had called friends from Auburn, and a prayer circle was outside the hospital praying for Darby. As word went out about Darby, prayers were being lifted for Darby across the world. Calls went out across all networks to pray for Darby. No one knew what was wrong, we just knew it was bad. From every corner of the globe, people stopped what they were doing and lifted prayers for Darby.

When they arrived at the hospital, John and Kelly's worst fears were realized.

"When we walked into the hospital, the doctor came to us and said, 'It isn't good at all,'" John said. "We asked what he meant, and he said, 'She's not going to make it.'"

Unbeknownst to anyone, Darby was born with Arteriovenous Malformation (AVM) in her brain stem. The AVM left blood vessels and arteries in her brain stem weak and vulnerable. On that day, Darby suffered a hemorrhage in her brain stem. There were no signs, no warnings, no indications anything was ever wrong. It was just a normal day…until it wasn't.

The doctors said that it was a miracle she lived as long as she did with this condition. But for John, Kelly, Brooks, Delaney and Brody, it was not long enough.

The day came when John and Kelly had to make a decision no parent should make. They had to make the decision to let Darby go and remove her from life support. After deciding to donate her organs, the family gathered around Darby, and prayed. Oh, how they prayed. Finally, even while Darby ran into the arms of Jesus, the family and friends were devastated. "Our hearts were broken, and lives shattered."

Little did we know what Darby would leave behind. Little did we know how God would use this special young woman's 18 years to impact so many lives. Little did we know then, that the reality of John 14 and Matthew 28 were so true. Little did we know how real those words would become as the Holy Spirit encircled that family. "I have such a burden of debt to so many people who poured themselves out to us," John said. He went on to explain how God touched him through this process. How God became real to him. How, through this horrific event, "I didn't know where to turn, so I turned to God and the scripture. I began to read the bible and read it differently and saw God's grace all through it." As John and Kelly O'Brien say time and again when asked about Darby, "This isn't our story. It is God's story, and we are a part of it."

We never know what kind of impact we make in this life. We never know how we are affecting people, even people we do not know. This was true for Darby. Her legacy lives long after her. Darby's reliance on her faith in God became so apparent to her parents and loved ones in the days and months after she went to heaven. A note found in her bible, a note she penned, made all of the difference to her parents and everyone who loved her. Her note said, "Why = No Faith."

How does one enjoy God while you are burying your child? How can we find solace in the heartache, gut wrenching pain that comes when you lose someone you love so dearly?

The same question is posed to the single dad who just got

laid off of his job because the company moved to another state or country. How do I take care of my family now? Or the family sitting in the parking lot of the hospital desperately wanting to say goodbye to their dad who is in his final stages before death.

The foreclosure papers are served, a diagnosis of cancer, the divorce papers, and the list goes on and on. The most difficult thing to do is to praise God in the trying times.

I am reminded of Job who was being tormented by Satan. Job was covered with sores "from the soles of his feet to the top of his head." (Job- 2:7) Job remained steadfast and when his wife was telling him to curse God, Job replied in 2:10, "…Shall we accept good from God and not trouble?"

When we are facing trying times in our lives, I offer these two observations.

First, do not ever compare what is trying for you to what is trying for someone else. Your bed of roses may be someone else's thorns. Because you do not understand the hardship of another does not mean it is not paralyzing to him or her. The fact of the matter is that we never really know someone else's struggles, their pain, or their heartache.

Secondly, instead of asking, "Why me?" (Remember, Darby wrote, "why = no faith.") when the trying times come, and believe me, they come to us all, ask yourself, "Why not me? Why should I be spared from the pain others are experiencing? Why should I be spared from the hardships of life?" Job was the most righteous man found on the earth, and he was not spared. King David had his son die. Solomon, the wisest man who ever lived, could not find happiness in his personal life. He had hundreds of wives and concubines and never found fulfillment.

Heartache, devastation, and trying times find us all. Your

tragedy may not be a death of a child. It may be the loss of a marriage, a job, or an illness. We cannot select the difficulties or control when they occur. We can only control our response to them. As Christians, we are not immune to the devastation life throws our way. When it comes, we need to draw closer to God in the midst of the storm.

John and Kelly O'Brien used their tragedy to spread the good news of Jesus to hundreds and thousands of people. They have used the death of their beloved Darby to impact lives all across the globe.

How do we enjoy God in the trying times? By keeping our eyes on him. By putting our attention on the love and Grace of Jesus Christ through whom all things are possible.

Paul tells us in Romans 8:38-39, some of the most beautiful verses he ever penned:

> "For I am convinced that neither death nor life, neither angels nor demons, neither the present nor the future, nor any powers, [39] neither height nor depth, nor anything else in all creation, will be able to separate us from the love of God that is in Christ Jesus our Lord."

When we are facing the trying times, that's when God is closest to us. He knows our pain; he knows our heartache, and he cries with us. Even when it feels impossible to enjoy God, when it feels like He is so far away from us, He is right there with us. We must keep our focus on him to help us to heal. How do we enjoy God during trying times? By taking our focus off of our pain and praise Him, and by knowing that nothing can separate us from the love of God that is in Christ Jesus.

7

Enjoying God in the Daily Struggles

Beep! Beep! Beep! Beep! Beep! The alarm is going off already. It feels like you just lay down and already the alarm is going off to get up and get going again.

It feels frustrating, defeating, and at times devastating. Life is so burdensome, so mundane, so painful at times. It takes all of our strength just to get out of the bed.

Alarm at 5:30 a.m., kids up at 6:00, breakfast for everyone, lunches made, a sip of coffee here, a sip there, and everyone is out the door. Just to do it again tomorrow, and the next day and the next day.

Life is so busy, so hectic that we barely have time to inhale, much less find time for God. And if we cannot find time for God, how in the world can we enjoy Him? How can we find the time to embrace His grace and love for us if we are so wrapped up in doing this or that that we forget to pray, we forget to read, we forget to praise Him? We have moved God to the margins of our lives. God desires to be in the body of the text of our lives, and we get so busy that God is relegated to the margins, where he is often forgotten or ignored.

Living in suburbia (reluctantly), I see it all too often with neighborhood after neighborhood, one on top of another. Cookie cutter houses have become modern caves. In the old South, where textile was king, mill villages sprang up everywhere. A textile mill was built near a water source to generate electricity. In order to have employees to work the mills, the owners built little villages, complete with churches, food stores, hardware stores and houses, around their mills. In many of the mill villages, there would be three churches built right next to one another. A Baptist, Methodist and Presbyterian church were each built identical to one another and right next to one another. The owners were wise enough to know that their employees needed spiritual nourishment to work well together.

These side-by-side, identical homes owned by the local textile mills were called mill villages here in the South. Today, we call them neighborhoods, or subdivisions. The floor plans are different, and the façade is improved, but they are still mill villages. Hundreds of houses built within feet of one another with three floor plans in the entire neighborhood. These expensive models of lifestyle have become bastions of recluse, or urban caves as I call them.

We see it all the time and just don't want to recognize it. In our world of social media, we have become extremely anti-social people. Marketing gurus of the planned subdivision have convinced prospective buyers of the utopia they are creating in this sea of cul-de-sac caves. Neighborhoods designed to maximize profits of developers present the allure of neighbors, friendly atmosphere where everyone loves one another and has each other's back.

The reality is less than 15 % of people living in neighborhoods know the names of their immediate neighbors, according to studies . And less than those know more than three people in their neighborhood.? We gather at neighborhood swimming pools only to stare at our phones instead of engaging with one another. We yearn for social impact and involvement and isolate ourselves in the midst of people. Modern society has caused many to believe that being busy is a decoration. But we are so busy being busy, we cannot stop to recognize the One who gives us everything.

Sitting in Sunday school a few months ago, we were trying to set a time when we could have an evening at our home to just get together outside of Sunday mornings. As we talked about it over and over, the number one reason people gave for not being able to come was, "We are just too busy." Ironically, most of us set our own calendar of events. We fill it with this and that and complain that we don't have time to do what we want.

Having a full calendar seems to be a badge of honor. We feel important if we are scheduled to the hilt. It makes us feel special if our time is being dictated, and we are stretched thin. Some even look down on those of us who find time to do – nothing. Even in this world of scheduling, I, for one, make time on my calendar to do nothing - time away, time to reflect, to breathe, time to just be. And it is during these times when I find God is the closest, when I'm not being pushed out by this meeting or that event. We can hear him when we are alone with Him.

The reality is this, we always find time for the things that are important to us. We find time to go to football games. We find time to watch our favorite TV show. We find time to grab a beer with the boys or have a girls' night out. We find time to take our kids here and there. But we cannot find time for God. We cannot find time to pray. We cannot find time to reflect and seek Him. We always have time for what is important to us. Always.

A long time ago, I attended a retreat for spiritual development. At this retreat, someone shared a story about priorities. In his story he shared this, "What do you think about? Where do you spend your money? Where do you spend your time? These are your priorities." Now thirty years later, those words still resonate with me.

As a writer, I spend a lot of time thinking about this story or that analogy for a book or article. I spend a lot of time researching and building the plot and a lot of money traveling for research. But those are all job related. We all need to focus on our jobs. There is no question about that. But when it comes to the priorities of our life, we have only one real choice: God, Spouse, Family …. Everything else.

We finally get home from work. There are bills to pay, grass to mow, animals to feed, homework to help with, baseball games to attend, supper to prepare and clean up from, get the kids ready for bed, and finally at 10:00 p.m., we have a minute to sit down and …. we fall asleep due to exhaustion.

Here's a personal story to help you see how I came to this point. Nineteen years ago, I was working in manufacturing. As the assistant plant manager, my duties were immense and at times overwhelming. As the new company was ramping up to begin full operations, I was working extremely long hours, 16 or more hours a day 6 days a week. It was not uncommon for me to turn in over 90 hours in a 6-day work week. As the father of young children, I was missing so much. I would arrive at the plant at 6:00 a.m. and seldom get home before midnight. My wife was such a trooper, handling everything at home with small children. One evening on a Tuesday, I came home around midnight, again, and she had dinner for me. She told me our son Ridge had taken his first steps that day. I was distraught that I'd missed it. A full 4 more days went by before I saw him walk! That was my awakening that my priorities were out of whack. There was only time for one thing - - work. No time for my family, my wife and certainly not God. Something had to be done. I immediately started looking for a new job.

Our day to day has become so full, we are running on empty. Our energy, patience, and love are empty because we are filling our days, and not our souls. We are filling our calendars and not our spirits. We are spending so much energy on our "activities" that we have nothing left to give to God.

Proverbs 3:9-10 says, "Honor the LORD with your wealth, with the first fruits of all your crops; [10] then your barns will be filled to overflowing, and your vats will brim over with new wine."

First fruits - we are to honor God with the first things, not the scraps. We honor God by keeping him in the body of the text and not the margins of our lives. In our hurried world, God is getting the scraps, the crumbs that fall from the table. We are spending our time, energy and money on everything except God. He wants the first fruits, and we give Him the leftovers. He wants to be front and center, not relegated to the margins.

While attending Erskine Theological Seminary in a class on Pastoral Care, the professor pointed out to us that throughout the decades of the 20th century, significant changes in the church mindset affected the role of pastor. He pointed out how the Pastor's Study has evolved into a church office, how the place designated for the pastor to spend time with God, to read, study, reflect and hear a message from God, has fallen by the wayside and the church office has replaced it. The duties of running the church have supplanted the importance of the church's role in the community. He continued to point out how even pastors have relegated God to the margins. The time we spend with God in prayer, study and in His word have been replaced with committee meetings, visiting the sick, and balancing check books.

I was convicted by his message and realized he was right. Since then, it has been a struggle to recognize God's place in my life and to ensure he is not relegated to the margins, rather as the main body of the paper.

How do we change this? The answer is simple to write but difficult to convince us to do. Put God first. Before anything else, praise Him. Before coffee, before breakfast, before getting the kids up, spend a few minutes with Him.

John Wesley, the founder of Methodism, felt that personal devotion was so important that he rose at 4:00 a.m. every day to spend two hours in devotion and prayer. While this may seem extreme, how many of us know people who get up at 4:00 or 4:30 to go to the gym? How many of us get up at 5:00 to go run four miles a day? How many of us get up early to go lift weights and spend an hour on the elliptical machine to make time for physical fitness but spend no time on our spiritual fitness?

Our days are full. Our lives are full. Many of us work several jobs just to make ends meet. We have a lifestyle that demands a certain income and to maintain that, we must work more and make more money. We don't mind sacrificing our time for more money. We don't mind sacrificing our time for longer vacations or another ball game. But for some reason, we cannot find time for God. I, too, am guilty of this. For as long as I can remember, I have had more than one job. Often times (as now), I have three jobs. For me, it is not about the money, although that helps, rather it is about the passion. My main job pays the bills; the others are driven by a calling to spread the word. Granted, the other two jobs are not full time, but they take time away from the family, from the rest of my life.

Micah 6:8 is a famous verse that many have in their homes. It is probably the only thing Micah is known for. The verse says, "What does the Lord require of you, but to do justice, love mercy and to walk humbly with your God." A simple phrase that when not just read but practiced will change your life.

How do we enjoy God in the daily struggles? We enjoy God by focusing our time, energy and mind on Him. We enjoy Him by spending time with Him. We enjoy God by being with God.

Life is so full of distractions that it takes real effort to spend quality time with God. It takes real effort to discover God. It takes real effort to enjoy God. But in this effort, we see the fullness of God. We feel his presence; we feel his grace.

Life is only mundane when God is not the center of everything we do. Life is only a struggle when God is not enjoyed. Life is only hard when we focus on ourselves and not on Him.

Do You Enjoy God? 12 Steps to Enjoying God Everyday

8

Finding Happiness

Where does happiness come from? How do we find true happiness? Every year Americans spend billions of dollars searching for happiness. According to the Market Data Enterprises, one of the few entities that tracks this information, self-help books and audio books accounted for over $9.9 billion in 2019. According to the CDC in the United States divorce rates are approaching 59 percent of all marriages. Suicide rates are increasing with over 48,000 people choosing this avenue in the US in 2019, according to the Centers for Disease Control.

Protests in the streets, looting, rioting, random killing of innocent people are all examples of discontent. As I write this, there is rioting in major cities all across America. Politicians are pointing fingers at one another, blaming one another for the terror in our cities. No one wants to take responsibility for the pain they are inflicting on one another.

The Guttmacher Institute reports that legal abortion kills more than 500,000 babies annually! Safe Horizon reports that human trafficking is affecting over 3 million children worldwide.

Drug addiction, alcoholism, pornography addiction, and more negatively impact children and families. People are seriously unhappy with their circumstances and with themselves at an alarming rate. The pain people feel in their personal lives is represented in the chaos they spread. People do not even know what gender God made them to be. And Senate Bill-145 in California allows pedophiles to walk free citing it as "discrimination against the LGBTQ young people" according to Senator Scott Weiner of the California State Assembly.

Have I gotten your attention? It's a gloomy picture for sure. Why are people so unhappy and sad? While I am not a therapist, I do observe, ponder, read and study some about the human condition, which is why I have a ministry to encourage people to enjoy God. I would like to share some of these observations and discuss how I believe YOU can find complete happiness.

Mind you, the phrase "complete happiness" does not in any way infer or guarantee you will no longer have difficult days or trying times. But it will show you how you can still find happiness, true happiness in the most difficult and trying times. No one can guarantee relief from sadness, tragedy or horrific accidents, but through the grace of almighty God, you can overcome and still find joy in the heartache.

Observation # 1: Happiness is found in the mirror not the window.

Happiness and contentment don't come from others. The other people in your life can enhance your happiness and joy, but they do not control it nor provide it to you. True happiness comes from within. It begins with how you see yourself. It begins with seeing yourself as someone that God breathed life into and created in His image for a reason and purpose.

As a Christian, I believe that my value and worth is found in Jesus Christ. The closer to Him I get, the more valuable I feel. The more valuable I feel, the happier I am. It is a circular harmony.

When we realize that we carry the image of God, that we are image bearers of the artist, it changes how we find happiness. The God of the universe and all there is cares about you individually and passionately. He created you for a purpose, and you are right here, right now to fulfill that purpose.

Happiness is found in the mirror, not the window. Stop looking for others to complete you or fulfill you. Look at yourself and know that you are created in the image of God. Happiness and joy are found in Him. By looking inward, we see the beauty of what God created. By looking inward, we begin to realize just how special we are, as God spoke through Jeremiah in 1:5 saying, "Before I formed you in the womb, I knew you. Before you were born, I set you apart." We realize that the same God that made the world with care and power made us! When we see that the same God that breathed life into Adam, breathed life into us. We see that the same God that put the stripes on the zebra, put the freckles on my face!

When we see this and embrace it as truth, we stop blaming others for our misery and realize that if God can love me – completely and enthusiastically- I can love myself. When the God of the universe finds you valuable, important and needed, how can you not find yourself valuable, important and needed? If God loves you, surely you can love yourself.

As noted above in the U.S. today, divorce rates are pushing 45% for first marriages. (second marriages are close to 60% and third marriages have a 73% failure rate). Think of that, who in their right mind would ever enter into anything that had a 45% failure rate? We would never invest our money in a stock with a 45% failure rate. We would never send our kids to a school that had a 45% drop out rate. We would never attend a church that has 45% of their congregation leaving. We would never accept a job where 45% of the people were fired! Why do we accept the marriage failure? What is the cause of the issue?

I am not a psychologist, but I am a theologian, and I see a strong correlation between people's happiness and the divorce rate. When we are looking for someone to *complete* us, or someone to *fulfill me* or someone to *make me whole*, we are destined for disappointment, heart break and failure. People today are entering marriage with an escape clause. Some say, "If I don't like her, I will just divorce her and move on," or "If he doesn't make me happy, I can always divorce him and find someone else."

Marriages today are focused on expecting the other person to *make them happy* rather than seeking happiness from within and with God. Happiness is not found in your spouse. Your spouse can bring you joy and happiness, but *true* happiness is found within and with your relationship with God.

When we see ourselves as loved by God, we find it easier to love others. The more we love others, the more we realize the love of God in us.

> 1 John 4:8-12 - [8] Whoever does not love does not know God, because God is love. [9] This is how God showed his love among us: He sent his one and only Son into the world that we might live through him. [10] This is love: not that we loved God, but that he loved us and sent his Son

as an atoning sacrifice for our sins. [11] Dear friends, since God so loved us, we also ought to love one another. [12] No one has ever seen God; but if we love one another, God lives in us and his love is made complete in us.

Look in the mirror, what do you see? You see someone who carries the image of God and someone God loves deeply. God *showed* His love for us. He demonstrated it for you. He sent His son for YOU.

Observation # 2: People look for happiness in things.

It may seem obvious to many, but to others it is not quite so obvious. When we look to fulfill our lack of self-worth based on our portfolio, job title, or position in society, we find that the tank we are trying to fill is endless. Happiness does not come from the things we acquire. Nicer cars, bigger trucks, finer clothing and perfect diamonds do not bring happiness. Bigger houses, fancier neighborhoods, and country club memberships do not bring happiness. They are veils that hide the pain we are covering. Seeking to acquire more is the modern elixir from the carpetbagger of old. Someone is selling a tonic to fix our pain, and the tonic is *more stuff*. The adage of the 1980's was, "He who dies with the most toys wins." And that mindset created a drive in people to acquire more and more stuff in an attempt to find value, meaning and a purpose.

On a recent trip to visit my son in Los Angeles, we did the tourist thing and went to Rodeo Drive in Beverly Hills. Walking down the street I was amazed at the amount of money parked along the sidewalk. There was close to twenty million dollars' worth of cars parked along the sidewalk. Models of Bentley, Rolls-Royce, Ferrari, Lamborghini, Range Rover, and so on lined the famous drive. There is nothing wrong with success or the spoils of success, in moderation. But we must be careful that we do not seek to acquire these things in hopes of them making us happy. In Philippians 4:12 Paul is reminding us to be careful with finding happiness in things. "I know what it is to be in need and I know what it is to have plenty, I have learned the secret of being content in any and every situation..." Paul's secret....is living in Christ in everything.

Many years ago, there was a gentleman in one of the churches I pastored, I will call him Jim. Jim came from a working-class family; his father worked in the local textile mill, and his mother stayed home. For some reason, Jim always felt inferior to his peers. His clothes were not as nice. While his friends drove cars, he walked. He was embarrassed that his family didn't have the finances that others seemed to have.

Jim had to drop out of school in the 8th grade to help support his family. He learned to be a brick and block mason. Soon he had his own business as a mason and was building hospitals, schools and colleges across the Southeast.

Jim made a decision that he would not be poor again, and he spent the next forty years working to achieve this...at the expense of his family. His wife and children seldom saw him because he worked so much. All of his free time was spent making money or investing money. For the better part of life, he worked and worked to make money.

He amassed a fortune, owned several homes scattered across the Southeast, owned vast real estate and many luxuries. His wife and children had little to do with him. When his kids became adults, they had a strained relationship with him at best. He was perplexed as to why. He couldn't understand why they were distant. As a grandfather, all he offered his grandkids was cash. No affection, no attention, only money. Jim felt all of his worth was found in his bank account. He was determined that his family would not have to do without as he did as a child and young adult. He was driven to not be poor, and he wasn't financially poor but was destitute in his relationships with family, friends and God.

Near the end of his life, he became estranged with most of his family. He just couldn't understand that love is not based on what you can provide for someone; it is based on how you make them feel. Because he never made his children feel valuable and loved, he died lonely, and rich. In the end, his kids got the money, but what they wanted was their daddy.

When we look for happiness in *things*, we learn, often too late, that the things we put our happiness in were shallow, fleeting and as the book of Ecclesiastes tells us, "…a chasing after the wind." (from 1:14).

Observation # 3: Happiness is achieved, not entitled.

In our world of instant gratification and short attention spans, I am seeing more and more people who want happiness, joy and satisfaction NOW! They don't want to do what it takes to achieve happiness; they want to obtain it. And they want it NOW! Right Now!

Happiness is achieved, not entitled. Day by day, minute by minute, we work to become and stay joyful. We do not wake up one day and discover that we are deeply happy with our lives and circumstances. We achieve happiness through a life of obedience to God and following His will. Whether alone or in a relationship, our happiness is something we control fully. As I have told my children time and again, "There are no bad days; there are only good days and great days, and we decide which one we will have."

Happiness is an attitude, an approach to life and life's circumstances. We decide how we will handle what life throws at us, and we handle it. When we get smacked down, we make a decision on how we will proceed.

When Jesus was facing trying times, what did he do? He went out into the wilderness to pray and seek God to help him through those tough times. He wasn't sad, he wasn't depressed or anxious. He was obedient and sought God for his joy and happiness. He realized that His fulfillment came from within. His fulfillment came from His intimate relationship with His Father and His God.

We see it so often with people who want today what took their parents 30 years to acquire. They have no concept of working for something, saving, investing and sacrificing to achieve their goal. They have no clue what it means to fail and then get up and try again. Many people are looking to others and the government to provide their happiness. They believe that happiness is brought to them because they exist. They do not see their value as being a child of God. They do not see value in themselves at all. When life doesn't go their way, they want to burn buildings, protest, and pout instead of trying to get better and be better.

As I write this, the Attorney General of California is telling the police to "consider if the looters *need* the items they are stealing before they arrest them." This whole mindset of excusing poor behavior is feeding the unrest and unhappiness in the people causing the pain. Making excuses for bad behavior does not mean the behavior is good. Bad behavior is bad behavior. Bad is bad, and good is good.

I remember, when coaching high school baseball, a fellow coach was in a discussion with a player who was upset that he wasn't getting enough playing time. The coach looked at him and as compassionate as possible said, "If you want to play more, get better."

What a great response! If you want to play more, get better. If you don't want to fail, get better. If you don't want to suffer sadness, get better. Happiness does not just come to us. We cannot obtain it; we can only achieve it. It does not come in other people, in things, bank accounts and possessions. It does not come from stealing, rioting or protesting. Happiness is not something we are entitled to, rather it is something we earn. Stop waiting on someone or something to make you happy. Go out and get it. Happiness is something we acquire by committing ourselves to the task of being happy. Happiness is a choice. Choose wisely.

The book of Ecclesiastes has been called one of the greatest pieces of literature ever penned. It is credited to Solomon, known as the wisest man who ever lived. All through Ecclesiastes, we see Solomon telling us that everything is meaningless. When we strive to please ourselves with work, labor, and material things, we are still empty. In chapter 2:10-11, Solomon writes:

> "I denied myself nothing my eyes desired;
> I refused my heart no pleasure.
> My heart took delight in all my labor, and this was the reward for all my toil.

¹¹ Yet when I surveyed all that my hands had done and what I had toiled to achieve, everything was meaningless, a chasing after the wind; nothing was gained under the sun."

What Solomon is saying here and throughout Ecclesiastes is to keep our focus on the right things, the things that matter. Nothing was gained under the sun. All of our work, all of our heart's desires are not where we find happiness. No, we can only achieve happiness through living a life worthy of the One whose image we bear. Embrace your image, know God put you right here, right now, for a reason. Serve Him, and your happiness will come, and it will come in measures indescribable.

Finding Happiness

Do You Enjoy God? 12 Steps to Enjoying God Everyday

9

Enjoying God in Worship

Worship is defined in the Oxford Dictionary as "the feeling or expression of reverence and adoration for a deity." Worship is indeed a deeply personal thing and one that is expressed in many different ways. During the Second Great Awakening at the turn of the 19th Century, the method of worship changed for a lot of people. With the rise of the Pentecostal movement, the way in which people expressed worship became paramount in their lives. No more was reverence necessary, but full emotional expression was encouraged. Throughout the 20th century worship has changed greatly and more so over the last thirty years. Worship has changed more dramatically during that time than perhaps at any time in history.

It wasn't that long ago that worship meant being quiet, reverent and stoic while in church. Everyone wore the best clothes they had and entered the church quietly because they were entering God's house. Before worship began, people filed into their seats and sat silently, or whispered to the person in the pew beside them. They used this quiet time to prepare their hearts for worship.

Music consisted of traditional hymns played on an organ and/or piano. Fanny Crosby, Isaac Watts, Charles Wesley and other hymn writers' songs were sung to melodies that have stood for centuries. The familiarity brought a sense of peace and contentment. The songs of their parents were ingrained in their soul and often found their way to their lips when hanging out the laundry or hoeing the garden. I remember vividly my grandmother singing hymns while she hung out laundry on her ever-present clothesline. And my mother as she watered plants in our house, heralded tunes from the old hymn books.

The act of worship was so well rehearsed that many could do it in their sleep - a greeting, sing a hymn, read some scripture from the Old Testament, sing another hymn, offer a prayer of concerns for the people, read an epistle. After this, the choir would sing a special song followed by the offering. Once the offering was done, another hymn was sung, and then a reading of the gospel message and a 20-minute sermon. Finally, a benediction occurred, and the people could leave, stand outside and shake hands, visiting with one another for twenty minutes and head to the restaurant or home.

Sometime during the 1980's this began to change and change drastically. What has become known as traditional worship began to go by the wayside and is now being replaced with *contemporary worship*. How we praise God has become more of a visual performance than an act of worship.

The irony is that the worship of the 1950's, '60's and 70's was considered "contemporary" at the time. Prior to this, many churches sang only the Psalms; hymns were considered sacrilegious because they were not scripture. Many churches refused to sing anything except Psalms or read from anything except the

King James Version of the Bible. Worship had changed.

What has happened to our worship? We have gone from ornate buildings of worship to store fronts, recycled buildings, and anywhere we can meet. What was once a place where craftsmen dedicated their lives to building the best they could for God has turned into constructing church buildings as cheaply as possible. Hymns have been completely abandoned for what is now called praise and worship music. Where has the enjoyment of God gone in the transformation? Has it gone at all?

As one person said in regard to contemporary music in church, "We have gone from hymns with lyrics that teach us about God, his grace and love to singing the same seven words eleven times." While this may be true in some cases, that does not mean they are not scripturally accurate or relevant.

I would like to be clear. I like contemporary worship, and I like traditional worship. But mostly, I like _authentic_ worship.

Worship is defined as expression of reverence of a deity. The word reverence means to "treat with deep respect" (Oxford Dictionary). I cannot help but wonder if this is what is happening today. I wonder if the respect is authentic. Honestly, I do not know. I wonder if there is more energy and emphasis placed on the light show and fake smoke than on the worship of God!

It is probably more individualized than I am making it out to be, meaning that in some churches, it is more authentic than others. It is always dangerous when you make blanket statements. More on that later, but for now, let's see how we can enjoy God through worship.

As an outdoor writer and active participant in many things outdoors, I have conversations regularly around campfires all across the world. I have heard every possible excuse for not attending worship services at a church. "This is my church," referring to the great outdoors, is the most common one I hear while in the wilds of creation. Second only to, "I can worship God anywhere." Followed closely by the third most-used excuse for not worshiping in church, "They [referring to church members] are all a bunch of hypocrites. Why would I want to be with them?" Perhaps the best excuse I have heard is, "I don't like the [stained glass] windows. They creep me out." I really didn't know what to do with that one.

Let's look at some of these to see why it is important to participate in worship and how we cannot fully enjoy God every day until we commit to worshiping him in a community of believers.

First, yes, church is full of hypocrites. People who say this are correct. We all are hypocrites; we all struggle with doing the right thing at times. The word hypocrite means, literally, mask wearer, as it is derived from the Greek word *hypokrisis*, which is an actor playing a part in a play, and the actor holds a large mask in front of his face. Is there anyone who does not from time to time put on a face in certain situations? Of course, we do.

Don't we act one way if we are meeting the governor of our state and another when talking to the tractor mechanic? We may value them equally, but the situation dictates a different response from us. Neither is less sincere; it is just a different mask for the situation.

Is there anyone of us who does not, from time to time, struggle with temptation and fail? Of course, we do. My question is what better place for hypocrites to be than at church? It is at church where the broken become healed. It is here that the struggles are eased, the pain reduced, and the burden shared. I can think of no better place for people to remove their masks than while worshiping the great God we serve! I can think of no greater place for falsehoods to be removed and for the struggles to be revealed than with a bunch of other strugglers.

Church is not for the perfect; it is for the broken. Church is for those who struggle, for those who need a boost or a lift to get through the week. It is a place where we can come and recover from whatever occurred the previous week and get ready for the one coming. It is where we are reminded that God is Love and that His love is real and for us. So, yes, churches are full of hypocrites. Why not come join us?

The book of Hebrews is one of the more encouraging books of the New Testament. I am sure some people do not see it quite that way, but I personally like the direct message the author sends time and again. In chapter 10, the author encourages people who are not attending church to reconsider their decisions. The New Living Translation puts it this way, "And let us not neglect our meeting together, as some people do, but encourage one another, especially now that the day of his return is drawing near." (Hebrews 10:25) There is no other verse that puts it so clearly and so encouragingly as does this one in verse 25. "Let us not neglect our meeting together….but encourage one another….." I especially like the last part, let us encourage one another. We attend worship with other believers so we can encourage one another, so we can enjoy singing to God, enjoy a word from God, and so we can *encourage* one another.

Secondly, when I hear someone say, "I can worship God anywhere," what I hear in that is, I don't want to break up my weekend to go sit in church for a few hours. What I hear is someone who is looking for an excuse *not* to attend church. Maybe they had a bad experience, maybe they just don't like the places they've visited. But mostly, I hear, "I don't understand what church is all about."

In short, yes, we can worship God anywhere. I do it daily, sitting at my desk, driving, hiking, fishing, sitting in tree stands while hunting. I worship God all the time. But in order to enjoy God to his fullest, we must experience God in corporate worship. We must do as the writer of Hebrews says, "And let us not neglect our meeting together, as some people do, but encourage one another...." By meeting together, we get encouragement, we get strength, and we get assurance that we are not alone in this battle.

Lastly, as a hunter and angler, I get to spend a lot of time in creation. I have been fortunate enough to travel to many places both remote and populated and have spent time with men and women from all over the globe. During these times, I have seen one commonality, and that is they are people who are in awe of creation. They are people who love God and who love the creation and all it has for us. During many of these conversations around campfires or while drifting silently along unnamed rivers, I have heard countless times, "This is my church."

But I would like to follow that with one simple question. Why? What is it about this place that makes it your church? What is it about this place that allows you to worship, to express reverence for a deity? Do you really *worship* here, or do you simply *admire* all God has created? Is it truly an expression of reverence? Or an excuse not to gather corporately?

I am the father of five children. We have been blessed to have five wonderful kids. (I am sure most parents say that.) They are all grown now and some have moved out, and others are not far behind, but through the years, I have tried to instill in them a few simple lessons.

One of these is to not confuse a reason with an excuse. If you can't cut the grass because it's hot, well, that's an excuse. But if you don't have a lawnmower, that could be a reason. If you don't take the trash out because you are still playing a video game, and you don't want to lose your place, well, that is an excuse. But if your leg is broken, and you can't walk, that is a reason not to take the trash out. There are big differences between an excuse and a reason. Too often in church today, we like to use an excuse and label it a reason.

Ms. Genell Wren used to lead the choir in the first church I pastored. She had a saying when we talked about why someone didn't come to church. Ms. Genell would say, "I guess they are out of peanut butter." The first time I heard her say it, I asked what she meant by that. "That excuse is as good as any. So, I guess they are out of peanut butter," she responded. She was so profound in that statement. If you are using an excuse not to go to church, well, you might as well be out of peanut butter.

When out in nature and saying, "This is my church," this is an excuse to not attend church; it's not really a reason. Perhaps, some people just don't like the church close by. Find another one. Perhaps some people were reared as a Wesleyan, and there are no Wesleyan churches nearby. Find a different church. Perhaps, the church only meets at 11:00, and some people want to be on the lake by 11:00. Adjust your time.

The Bible is clear in this point in Hebrews 10:25. "And let us not neglect meeting together, as some people do, but encourage one another......"

Worship today is far different from what I grew up attending. I can't say I like it, nor do I dislike it; it is just different. But one fear I do have is I see more and more churches turning away from the traditions that carried them for two thousand years. There seems to be more emphasis on the coffee room than the accurate teaching. There seems to be more concern about the greeters in the parking lot than the altar.

While preparing for this chapter, I have been visiting churches every week - Baptist, Wesleyan, Non-denominational, Methodist, Presbyterian, Lutheran and a few I am not sure if they even know who or what they are. One common theme is resonating throughout these new 'styles" of worship. There seems to be a lot more emphasis on the "presentation" of worship than the content of worship. One well-known church in our area with several satellite campuses seems convinced that extreme volume, lasers and fake smoke enhance the worship. But each time I've been, they sing the same songs and have a similar sermon. There is no depth to the presentation. They are great at getting seekers, but not so good at discipleship.

In an effort to relate to the millennials, churches have moved and removed a lot of traditional churches. How does the altar offend people? Where are the symbols of Christianity within the church? Why do we not proclaim who we are as Christians to all who visit?

At one mega-church I visited, I asked one of the greeters, "Where are the Christian symbols?"

She beamed and proclaimed proudly, "Oh, we don't have any. We don't want people to know they are in a church when they come here. We want them to feel comfortable." I didn't go back.

How people do church is changing. There is no getting away from that fact. But how we worship must not be replaced with *why* we worship. We worship to draw closer to our God. If we lose our focus on that, we are just having a party to feel good about ourselves and not focusing on Him. Sadly, in many venues today, it is more of a feel-good party and not worship. We must be careful we do not fall into the trap Paul warned about in 2 Timothy chapter 4

> "...I give you this charge: 2 Preach the word; be prepared in season and out of season; correct, rebuke and encourage—with great patience and careful instruction. 3 For the time will come when people will not put up with sound doctrine. Instead, to suit their own desires, they will gather around them a great number of teachers to say what their itching ears want to hear. 4 They will turn their ears away from the truth and turn aside to myths. 5 But you, keep your head in all situations, endure hardship, do the work of an evangelist, discharge all the duties of your ministry." (2 Timothy 4: 1-5)

When we worship, we should do so honestly, as Jesus told us in the great parable of the woman at the well.

> 23 Yet a time is coming and has now come when the true worshipers will worship the Father in the Spirit and in truth, for they are the kind of worshipers the Father seeks. 24 God is spirit, and his worshipers must worship in the Spirit and in truth." (John 4: 23-24)

At the end of the day, if you are drawn closer to God in a modern style of worship, praise be to God. If you are drawn closer to God in a traditional style of worship, praise be to God. The method is not as important as is the sincerity and authenticity. Be real, be genuine and participate every chance you can.

True authentic worship is what matters, whether you do it traditionally, contemporarily or some mixture. Do it in spirit and truth and be authentic in your heart as you bring praise to God.

As we look at Enjoying God Every Day, let me ask, if we omit worship, can we enjoy God? If we do not join with other believers and share in corporate worship, can we fully live the premise of the meaning of life? What is the chief end of mankind? "To glorify God and to enjoy Him forever." Worshiping with fellow believers is one way we can arm ourselves against the evil forces that are pulling us away from God and where we can prepare to enjoy Him daily.

Enjoying God in Worship

10

Enjoying God in the Outdoors

As a young man in my early teens, I was bitten by a strange bug. It didn't seem that serious at first. What appeared to be a minor ailment grew into a serious infection. My mother and father, at first, were complacent to its effects, but as the infection grew, their concern matured. After many discussions and attempted antidotes, they learned there was no antiseptic for its properties.

Gradually the infection ran through my veins. The longer is remained, the more immune I became to remedies. The infection caused a voracious thirst - for knowledge in everything that involved exploring, fishing, hunting, outdoors, living off of the land, etc. Every book in our local library on Daniel Boone, John Muir, Mountain men, Davy Crockett, Lewis and Clark, Saxton Pope, Robert Ruark, Archibald Rutledge, Havilah Babcock and others was read and re-read. Every book on survival, self-reliance became consumed. I began subscribing to outdoor magazines. *Sports Afield*, *Outdoor Life* and *Field and Stream* became common sights in my home.

Around the age of fourteen, while reading the *Outdoor Life* magazine from cover to cover for the umpteenth time, I noticed an advertisement for the *Outdoor Life* Book Club. The advertisement read that if I mailed in one dollar, they would send me 10 books on the outdoors. All I had to do was buy two books within a year at full price.

I ran to my mother, asked for an envelope and mailed in my dollar. Within a few week, a package arrived. It contained ten outdoor books that I devoured over and over again. I read and re-read *How to Track and Find Game, Whitetail Deer Hunting, Small Game Hunting, The Outdoor Eye,* and others. None of the books escaped my intrigue. Not being from an outdoor family, I would literally take these books into the field and read what they said and try it out.

Through these books, I learned to discern the difference between squirrel tracks and rabbit tracks. I understood how to see wildlife in the forest. I began to learn how game moved across the landscape. These books and countless hours taught me about nature, animals, and God's creation. To add to the collection, I bought two books during the year. One was a Jack O'Connor book on shotguns and the other *Flyfishing* by Tom McNalley.

I was not aware then, and frankly, it was several decades later when I came to realize what occurred. God touched me with a special affection for His creation. Nothing in the creation goes underappreciated. Everything - from the salamander in the creek, to the fading autumn leaves gives, to giant pike and beautiful whitetail deer - brings my heart joy.

I am fortunate in that I make a considerable amount of my living in the outdoors. Working for the USDA and as an outdoor writer and podcaster, I get the opportunity to spend close to 300 days a year in the outdoors. It is as if God blessed me with the ability to make a living doing some of the things I love most, enjoying God in the outdoors.

I recognize that the wilds do not appeal to everyone. Indeed, many people are afraid of the forest and woodlands. People not accustomed to the out-of-doors have difficulty finding solace there. Just as I am uncomfortable in large cities, they, too, are uncomfortable in the wildlands I so long for. But stay with me for a bit, and let's see how we can enjoy God in the outdoors.

The outdoors may mean one thing to me and something else entirely to you. That's okay. To you, it could be the garden on your balcony or a city park. It could be a slow walk along a river or a visit to the local zoo. It is all a matter of perspective and opinion. Regardless of where you find God in the outdoors, it doesn't change the point that God is there and wants to be enjoyed through his creation.

I am a firm believer that God created all of the majesty for us to enjoy and to be drawn to Him through his creation. Remember in Genesis chapter 1:3, "And God said, 'Let there be light,' and there was light." God spoke, and it was so. God said, and from nothing everything came into being. I believe that God created the world and everything in it for us. We are created in God's image. We are like God in will, intellect, and authority. Consequently, God gave us dominion over creation. God intended for us to not only benefit from creation, but to enjoy his creation.

The world is full of so many beautiful places, plants and animals. I am always amazed at the creative power of God, and his ability to create from nothing something as beautiful as Earth. Fortunately, I have been able to travel across this country a few times, by air and by automobile. Each time, I find myself astounded at the beauty of our great land and the creativity of God.

How do we enjoy God in the outdoors? It begins with being quiet and listening. We are listening for the sounds of nature, but more, we are listening to the voice of God. Pat Mingarelli, a friend of mine who has the ministry, *Visual Bible Verse of the Day*, emphasizes solitude and the importance of solitude to enjoy God. He shares that one of the reasons for solitude is so we can hear God speak. Too often we are in a world of noise and confusion. We are so busy being busy that we cannot hear God speak. Our prayer life is full of us talking, giving God a list of wants and needs and then saying good-bye. When we are quiet with God, we are better able to hear him speak to us. By taking some time to be alone with God, we are more apt to discern what His desire for us really is and what he wants for us.

Years ago, one of the finest gentlemen I have ever known, Alan Reid shared with me a story of when he was a child. He grew up with a wood cook stove in his family home. It was his job to get the wood in every morning so his mother could start the stove and cook breakfast.

One day while I was visiting, Alan told me how they got their wood for the kitchen stove. He began, "The full moon of March, my daddy would take me and my brother into the woods to find a big pine tree. He selected the tree, and my brother and I would begin sawing down the tree. We had a two-man crosscut saw and we would get as close to the ground as we could to cut the tree down.

When the tree fell, Daddy would take his axe and start cutting the limbs off of the tree. Limbs big enough to burn in the kitchen he would stack up for us, the rest he used to build a fire for us. My brother and I would start bucking the tree into ten-inch blocks. We cut the entire 80' tree into ten-inch blocks.

One day we were resting, and Daddy asked if we needed to sharpen the saw. My brother said, 'No we got it.' And we worked and worked and worked. Several hours into it, Daddy offered to give us a break. Taking the saw, he sat on a stump and began sharpening the saw. Tooth by tooth he went with his file on the saw blade. Turning it over, he began on the other side until the entire five-foot saw was sharpened. He then got on one side of the tree and began sawing the tree into ten-inch blocks. The saw almost flew through the tree. My brother and I stared at one another. Daddy got up, handed us the saw and said, 'Boys, sometimes the best use of your time is to stop and sharpen your saw instead of fighting a dull one.'"

Since Alan Reid shared with me that story, I have come to recognize when my saw gets dull, and I stop and take the time to sharpen my saw. When life gets hectic, and time with God is getting lost in the shuffle, my saw gets dull. When work is overwhelming, the back is hurting, and time seems stretched too thin, my saw gets dull. When the priorities are out of whack, I know it is time to stop, sit on the stump and sharpen my saw.

I find the best way for me to sharpen my saw is to find solitude in the outdoors. Listening to the sounds of nature calms my soul. The constant call of the whippoorwill on a summer evening, the echo of a loon on a remote lake, the desperate bugle of a bull elk all remind me that God is so loving and gracious.

For you it may be going to the lake for a day, a hike at the park or sitting by the shore. Whether it is familiar or foreign – the outdoors is a place God is revealed through his creation. It is a place where, when we look, we can see the awesomeness of God in all of the things around us. Flowers, trees, ducks, pigeons, elk, deer, the green grass, and calm waters all tell us that God is full of love, beauty, grace and gives assurance that "What has been will be again, what has been done will be done again; there is nothing new under the sun." (Ecclesiastes 1:9) God is the same, yesterday, today and forever.

The comfort of God in the outdoors is something all of us can benefit from. The joy God brings to us in his creation is magnificent.

The only balm for my ailment that infected me so long ago has been the fresh air of the mountain, the rippling of a stream, the parading of elk through a valley and the honking of geese on their way South. I am infected with a passion for the outdoors, and I am thankful to God for giving me this condition. It is because of Him that I get to enjoy his creation on a daily basis. It is where I thrive in my soul, and where I get to know God intimately. It is my sanctuary.

What is your sanctuary? Where do you enjoy God? If you have not considered the outdoors, consider going outside. Watch a fire, gaze at the stars, hike a trail, float a river, or drive in the country. And when you do, pause and look, but mostly listen. God speaks to us through his creation. When you listen, you are more likely to hear him as he reminds you how much he loves you and wants only the very best for you.

Enjoying God in the Outdoors

11

Recognizing God in Your Life

Admittedly, this may be the most difficult chapter to write. Questions abound about this topic. Before diving into it, I have to admit, the points listed here are not the definitive answer to this and many questions that surround this topic. How do we recognize God?

I have often envied Adam and Eve. Not only did they live in paradise, but the scripture tells us in Genesis, Chapter 3, that they talked with God and walked with him in the Garden. Can you imagine how it would feel to actually walk with God and talk with him? God asking about your day, "How was your day Pete?" And having his ear as you poured out your burdens on him as you strolled through the garden.

As a pastor, I am often associated with having received a *calling* into ministry. There are a few other careers where this term is used, but not many. Most people choose their career based on what they either enjoy doing or something they are inherently good at doing. A friend of mine, when asked why he became a math teacher said, "I have always been good at math, so I figured

I could either teach math or become an engineer, and I didn't want to do that, so here I am."

Pastors and others are often asked about their calling. When being interviewed for a position within a church, one of the first questions asked by the committee to a prospective pastor is "Can you tell us about your calling?" And having been asked this on many occasions, I find that each time I retell the story of my calling, it is a little different. There are different details, and some things are left out for brevity. How do you explain to someone who has never received a calling, what your calling is about? How can you tell someone what your relationship with God is like? What are the words you choose when asked to "share one of your most intimate moments with the panel here, and we will try and understand it?"

In short, a person cannot (at least I have not been able to) convey his or her calling to anyone else. It is personal and belongs to the individual uniquely. I can empathize with someone about his or her calling. I can even sympathize with someone about his or her calling, but I will not be able to fully understand what one's calling is nor what it means to that person. When God calls someone, he calls that individual uniquely and specifically with what he or she wants and needs to hear.

How do we know when God is speaking to us? How are we sure it is God and not Satan disguised as God? The deceiver is excellent at disguising himself as God and letting us believe it is from God, when in fact it is Satan. What are some things someone can do to vet the source and gain some level of certainty that what he or she is sensing, feeling and believing is indeed from God himself?

One of the ways is recognizing that the Hollywood depiction

of Satan is not the biblical depiction of Satan. If you remember in Genesis 3, when Satan took the form of the serpent, Eve was not afraid of him. She didn't run; she didn't scream and climb onto a chair and yell, "Adam, kill it!" No, she talked with the serpent. And what did the serpent do? He didn't threaten Eve. He confused her. He made her question God.

> "Did God really say, 'You must not eat from any tree from the garden'?"
> The woman said to the serpent, "We may eat fruit from the trees in the garden, 3 but God did say, 'You must not eat fruit from the tree that is in the middle of the garden, and you must not touch it, or you will die.'"
> 4 "You will not certainly die," the serpent said to the woman. 5 "For God knows that when you eat from it your eyes will be opened, and you will be like God, knowing good and evil" (Genesis 3:1-5).

In Genesis 3:4, the serpent used Eve's curiosity to confuse her, "You will not certainly die," Satan said. When we start to recognize God and all of his goodness, that's when Satan begins to work on us to confuse us. It is then that he attacks us and tries to get us to question God and what God's motives really are. As we draw closer to God, we see that recognizing him can become more difficult. The closer we get, the more determined Satan is to confuse us.

How does God reveal himself to us? Actually, there are several ways in which he chooses to reveal himself.

In God's divine wisdom, he created the scriptures to help us to better understand him. He did this so that we could have an intimate relationship with him. He did this so we would know Him and know Him intimately. It is God's greatest desire to have a close relationship with us, and let's face it that is hard to do if we do not recognize Him. It is hard to do when we question him and his motives.

How does God reveal himself to us? As we have already read in Genesis 3, he walked with Adam and Eve. It was easy for them to recognize him. Later, the scripture tells us that when the Garden was closed for good, the ability for human beings to "see" God was lost.

Just because the ability to "see" God is lost, it does not mean that God does not reveal himself to us. There are many ways in which God reveals himself to us, ways in which we can recognize him. We will look at four ways in which God reveals himself and begin with what many believe is the primary method God reveals himself to us - through his word.

The Holy Bible is God's word to us. While this may seem cliché, it is in fact true. God uses his living word to help us recognize how he is active in our world and in the lives of his children. Let's look and see how this is true.

"...I am God, and there is no other; I am God, and there is none like Me. I make known the end from the beginning, from ancient times, what is still to come. I say, 'My purpose will stand, ...'" (from Isaiah 46:9-10).

In 2 Timothy we are told, "[16]All Scripture is God-breathed and is useful for teaching, rebuking, correcting and training in righteousness, [17] so that the servant of God may be thoroughly equipped for every good work." (2 Timothy 3:16-17)

Much has been written about whether many of the events that are documented in the Bible are actual facts, metaphors, hyperbole, antidotes, similes, and more. Are the scriptures actually true? Are the scriptures inspired by God? Were they dictated by God? Was it merely men and women who wrote down how they felt, and what they saw? There are so many questions, and it can be a deep dark hole that will swallow us up in conjecture and innuendo. Rather than fall into that here and now, suffice it to say, that I believe as John Wesley, the father of Methodism, said far better than I could, "We know, 'All Scripture is given by inspiration of God,'..." For those who believe, and many who do not, the Holy Bible is God's word for his people. It is His manner of communicating with His creation.

Again, refer to 2 Timothy 3:16-17 – "All Scripture is God-breathed and is useful for teaching, rebuking, correcting and training in righteousness, 17 so that the servant of God may be thoroughly equipped for every good work." All scripture is God breathed...it is given by God to His people and is necessary and useful for all things. In short, the Bible contains all things necessary to see God, to hear God and to experience God in unique and powerful ways.

The modern debate on whether or not the scripture is without error is, in my estimation, to miss the point entirely. Believers agree that God inspired the word and gave the message to his scribes who then wrote it down. God, knowing this would be His word for all creation, was careful enough to ensure its accuracy so that the message he intended is not missed, and the grace is expressed completely and thoroughly.

As 1 John tells us in 4:19, "We love [God] because he first loved us." Our ability to love God and one another is found in the scripture and is nestled in the understanding that our ability to love is because He first loved us. Moreover, our ability to recognize God's action in our lives is also found in scripture. The scripture is alive and reaches us where we are when we need it most.

A second manner in which God reveals himself to us and enables us to recognize him is through our conscience. What is conscience? For believers, we see the conscience as the Holy Spirit that lives in us. From the moment we accept Christ as our personal savior the Holy Spirit begins a work in us. In John 14:15-17, Jesus is talking to his disciples and telling them,

> If you love me, keep my commands. **16** And I will ask the Father, and he will give you another advocate to help you and be with you forever— **17** the Spirit of truth. The world cannot accept him, because it neither sees him nor knows him. But you know him, for he lives with you and will be in you.

The Holy Spirit is the third person of the trinity that is God with us. In short, God loved us enough to remain with us even after Jesus ascended to the father. In John 14:16-17, Jesus says the Holy Spirit is given "to help you and be with you forever…the Spirit of truth." Our conscience is our compass; it lets us know right from wrong. When we begin to go astray, when we struggle with choices, when we seek guidance, it is the Holy Spirit of God that he instilled in our hearts that guides us.

Do you want to be able to recognize God and when he is with you? Consider your conscience is exactly that. It is the Holy Spirit of God that is guiding you and leading you to make the right decisions. It may not be easy, or popular, but it is right. Often times, we are more concerned about being right than we are over

Recognizing God in Your Life

doing the right thing. But our conscience tells us that doing the right thing is always the right choice.

A third way in which God reveals himself to us is through Jesus Christ. Perhaps the most glorious element of our God is that he loved us enough to come to us in the form of Jesus to show us the way. John puts it so eloquently in the preamble to his gospel when he says,

> In the beginning was the Word, and the Word was with God, and the Word was God. 2 He was with God in the beginning. 3 Through him all things were made; without him nothing was made that has been made. 4 In him was life, and that life was the light of all mankind. 5 The light shines in the darkness, and the darkness has not overcome it…
> 9 The true light that gives light to everyone was coming into the world. 10 He was in the world, and though the world was made through him, the world did not recognize him. 11 He came to that which was his own, but his own did not receive him. 12 Yet to all who did receive him, to those who believed in his name, he gave the right to become children of God — 13 children born not of natural descent, nor of human decision or a husband's will, but born of God. 14 The Word became flesh and made his dwelling among us. We have seen his glory, the glory of the one and only Son, who came from the Father, full of grace and truth (John 1: 1-5, 9-14).

I emphasize verse 11, *"He came to that which was his own, but his own did not receive him."*

Personally, I believe this is THE verse that John builds his entire gospel on. John will spend the next 17 chapters trying to address this one verse. Jesus was with God in the beginning, from the onset of creation, he was there. Jesus put the stripes on the zebra and the trunk on the elephant. He planted the vines in the garden and colored the birds of the air.

Then one fateful day, God came to Jesus and said, "I need you to go and show them the way back home."

The man Jesus is a historical fact. It has been proven time and again that he did indeed live. Christians believe that not only did he exist, but that he was fully God and fully man, that he lived on earth, without sin. They believe he came as a child from the Virgin Mary and taught the people of His day and beyond how we are to live. Jesus gave us the example of how we should live. The gospel of Mark helps us to understand this in chapter 12:28-31:

One of the teachers of the law came and heard them debating. Noticing that Jesus had given them a good answer, he asked him, "Of all the commandments, which is the most important?" 29 "The most important one," answered Jesus, "is this: 'Hear, O Israel: The Lord our God, the Lord is one. 30 Love the Lord your God with all your heart and with all your soul and with all your mind and with all your strength.' 31 The second is this: 'Love your neighbor as yourself.' There is no commandment greater than these."

In these short verses Jesus teaches us what is most important. What matters most...Love God, love one another.

God sent Jesus here to help us to experience him fully. God is revealed to us through the person of Jesus Christ. How can we recognize God? Look at the example of Jesus. What did Jesus do?

In 1990 at Calvary Reformed Church in Holland, Michigan, a youth leader named Janie Tinklenberg began a grassroots expression to help her youth understand the meaning from the 1896 book from Charles Sheldon titled *In His Steps* and subtitled *What Would Jesus Do?* Ms. Tinklenberg had bracelets made with WWJD printed on it. The rest, as they say, is history. The bracelets spread like wildfire all over the world and even today, the WWJD phrase has premediated society. Many variations and copy-cat sayings on bracelets have emerged since then. But the message is the same. "What would Jesus do?" is as accurate a question today as when it was first ever asked. God is revealed in the person of Jesus Christ. He loved all, he forgave those who harmed him and betrayed him. He healed the sick and comforted the hurting. Want to recognize God? Look to Jesus. He is right there.

Finally, God reveals himself through others. Allow me to share a personal story. This story occurred over a 6-year time period, but I will not drag you through the entire time, just the highlights.

In November 1985, I was sitting in a deer stand hunting. It was one of those hunts where you are there physically but not really there mentally. My mind was tormented with confusion and fear. As I sat there, I began to pray.

"God, I am not sure what to do. I am afraid. I have no education. I cannot speak clearly. I have no money and a terrible job. What am I supposed to do?"

Before I continue, let me say clearly that I have often, and frankly still often, balk when someone says, "God spoke to me and said…" I have seen too many times where people use that phrase to manipulate others for personal gain. So, I say this with a lot of fear and trembling.

As I prayed that prayer that day, I heard, as clearly as I have ever heard any voice from someone speaking to me, these words, "Throw away your running shoes and open your deaf ears."

It was so clear and so precise. I immediately began to look around for someone standing there or near me. I was startled and said, "Who is that?" Then, I heard it again, as clearly and as distinctly as anything, "Throw away your running shoes and open your deaf ears."

I had no idea that was God speaking to me, and I was afraid. So afraid, I got down from my deer stand and went home.

My mind was racing. Fast forward to late February or early March of 1986 (I am not sure which it was). One Saturday morning, for no real good reason, I went to see my pastor. This was not something I had ever done before. I knew him but was not close to him at all. In fact, I had never really spoken to him before. As I walked into his carport, he was working on a wooden boat he was building.

"Good morning, Preacher," I said. As I walked toward him, he was putting some varnish on the boat.

"Good morning! What brings you here?" he asked.

"I wanted to talk to you for a minute if you have it," I said.

"Sure, come on in. What is it about?" he asked.

I just stood there because I really didn't know why I was there. I just went with no agenda or topic to discuss. I just felt an urging to go.

We stood there in silence for what felt like hours as he puffed on his pipe and spread the varnish on the boat. Finally, he broke the silence and asked, "When are you going to stop running from God and listen to him?"

"What do you mean?" I asked.

"You know what I mean. God has been calling you into the

ministry, and you won't listen," he insisted.

I stood there......finally saying, "I guess that is what I came to talk to you about. I am not sure what is going on here."

For the next several hours, we talked about what I was feeling, what I sensed and how to go about it all.

God used my pastor to reveal Himself to me in a profound way.

The next week, we made a phone call to the district superintendent of our district. As a United Methodist, there is a process. I made an appointment to go see the district superintendent. It was March 1986. We spoke. I went to meetings, saw people, answered a ton of questions, took psychological tests and more examinations.

One day in April, I received a phone call from the district superintendent, and he informed me that I was being assigned a church in June to serve as pastor.

Throughout my life, I have seen how God has used other people to reveal himself to me. Time and again, a word or a touch from someone and I knew God was there. In hospital rooms, funeral homes, and across dinner tables, God has used those around me to show me his love, his grace and his magnificence.

Indeed, I would surmise that outside of scripture, God uses those around us more often to reveal himself to us than any other manner.

How do we recognize God? By looking for him. Look for him in the eyes of others. Look for him in the birds, the trees and sky. Look for him in his word. It is easy to find something when we are looking for it. We don't just stumble upon God. We find him when we are looking for him.

12

Conclusion

Q: What is the chief end of mankind?

A: The chief end of mankind is to glorify God and to enjoy Him forever.

This simple question from the Westminster Shorter Catechism changed my life. When I read those words over seven years ago, it sent me on a journey to try every day to ENJOY GOD! When I first read those words, I assumed that portion of the answer was attributed to the eternal time when I am with God in his presence in Glory. However, after giving it significant thought, I realize that no, I can and should enjoy God today, NOW! Why would I wait until I die to enjoy God fully? Why would I wait until my life is over to experience his fullness and greatness? I can and should enjoy him now.

Making a conscious decision to enjoy God every day has made me a better husband to my wife. It has made me a better father to my children. A better friend, better colleague, and better person overall. No longer do I see the bad in things, but only God's goodness. Only God's greatness. Only God's wonderful love and guidance.

Like many people in this world, I have my struggles. I have weaknesses and areas where I struggle. However, since making the decision to *enjoy God every day*, I have seen most of those struggles fade away. Areas of temptation are gone. Things that brought tension, strife, and stress are released.

By focusing on *enjoying* God, I learned that I cannot be sad while praising him. By taking the attention off of myself and focusing on praising God and enjoying him, my days are now great, even when things don't go how I would hope or how I planned. Giving thanks to God for all that is good takes away the stress and anxiety and helps me to see that God truly is *good*, and he truly does love me and want what is best for me.

I hope as you read this book, you, too, find comfort and peace in knowing that God's love for you is real. His compassion is sincere, and His grace is sufficient for all things. I pray that you, too, will find a way to enjoy God every day.

Conclusion

Do You Enjoy God? 12 Steps to Enjoying God Everyday

About the Author

Pete Rogers earned his BA from the University of South Carolina and a Masters in Divinity from Erskine Theological Seminary. Over twenty-one years ago Pete began his writing career. He has published over one thousand articles, and four thousand photographs for numerous publications. And is the author of six books to date. He is a member of several national and regional writing organizations and has served as president and chairman of the board for the South Carolina Outdoor Press Association.

Pete is the founder host of Christian Outdoors Podcast where they "Discuss all things outdoors and how we can enjoy God every day." It is available on all podcast outlets.

He is the husband of Susan Rogers and the proud father of Hannah, Alex, Ruth, Ridge and Dinah, currently he and his wife reside in Taylors, SC.

If you would like to have him speak at your church or next event, he can be contacted at; pete@christianoutdoors.org or through his website, www.christianoutdoors.org

Do You Enjoy God? 12 Steps to Enjoying God Everyday

Made in the USA
Monee, IL
24 September 2021